THE JAM
AND
OTHER
RELATIONSHIPS

Russ Hayton

Published by

MELROSE
BOOKS

An Imprint of Melrose Press Limited
St Thomas Place, Ely
Cambridgeshire
CB7 4GG, UK
www.melrosebooks.co.uk

FIRST EDITION

Copyright © Russ Hayton 2013

The Author asserts his moral right to
be identified as the author of this work

Cover designed by Simon Mortimer

ISBN 978-1-907732-80-5

Printed and bound in Great Britain by:
Mimeo Ltd, Huntingdon, Cambridgeshire

FSC
www.fsc.org
MIX
From responsible
sources
FSC® C019549

CONTENTS

PROLOGUE   **1**
  October 1995   **1**
    Confusion   1

THE JOURNEY   **2**
  June 1996   **2**
    Guines   2
    Beuzeville   3
    Decision   5
    Rennes   8
    Success   9
    The Jam!   10
    Trémorel   11
    October 1995   13

PERTURBATIONS   **15**
    Oh boy, today!   15
  November 1995   **17**
    Contemplation   17
    Poitiers   18
    Perfection   25
    Family   32
  Rejection   **33**
    Relationships with Women, Relationships with Blokes   33
    A Ploy   35
    To Carcassonne   38
    Sublimation   40
    Air in the Square   41
    Good Feelings   42
    Villemoustousou   45

Mission Completed   47

Beautiful People   49

Toulouse   50

A Most Beautiful Place   53

December 1995   **55**

Happy Christmas   55

Chateauneuf du Pape   56

January 1996   **58**

And a Happy New Year   58

Cherries at Bonnieux   63

February 1996   **63**

Doctor, Doctor   63

Par le Pont d'Avignon   64

Nipples   67

March 1996   **67**

Vacillation   67

Gonzalo Plays Flute   69

Almost   75

Vaucluse   76

Carpentras   76

BOY   79

Smoking Women   79

Breakfast at Les Halles   82

Jean Luc   88

Maulecéne   88

Kisses   88

Gap   89

Josephine   89

Long Split Skirt   90

Cin Valley   92

Briançon   93

Italy   94

Torino   95

Alessandria   95

Casteggio   96

Moonies at 150   98

Hell's Angels   99
Trieste   104
Hayton's First Law   **106**
Obelesco   106
The Corkscrew Factor   108
Slovenia   113
Sezana   115
Istanbul – Not Quite, but Nearly   119
Innerbraz, Austria   124
Schaffhausen   125
Going Home Blues   128
Metz   129
Charlesville Mezieres   130
Cambrai   132
St Omer   134
Dominic - CAFÉ - L'EXCALIBUR - S'OMER   134

RELATIONSHIPS   **145**
Josephine   145
R   146
Trixie   148
Charlie   149
Return   150

EPILOGUE ONE   **152**
Pertinacity   152
Return to Avignon   167
La Grippe   168
To Françoise in Toulouse   168
Coutances - with Cathedral   169
Souillac   170
Rennes-Bruz-Chartres de Bretagne and 'La Space Exposition'   170
Toulouse, Françoise and Failure   171
Gaillac   172
Alban   172
Roquefort   173

Sebastien in Saint Affrique   173
Avignon for the Third Time   175
Villeneuve   176
Le Puy   178
Peyrat au Chateau   180
Mid-Channel   182
Good Advice   183

EPILOGUE TWO   **185**
Avec Françoise, il y a t'espoir. C'est tout?   185
Diana   189
Crete   **190**
Florence   190
Anna   192
Camel   194
Monday   198
Yoga   198
"Dave, read my fucking book."   200
Alfa Class F   203
IF   **205**

PROLOGUE

October 1995

Confusion

God!

What am I doing? Look at this bloody mess. Paper rearranged for the nth time. Credit cards not paid. Can't find the blue one...

Three cult titles on a card: Hitchhiker's Guide to the Galaxy, The Last Chance to See Douglas Adams, Precious Present Johnson *– not even bought them.*

"Lighten up," she said. How can I lighten up, damn it? She's standing between me and more despondency.

Those three titles – I should have read them by now. And The Dice Man. *Not a chance. Too busy with work and delusions of grandeur. I should be famous by now – highly regarded.*

I've had enough of this humiliation. Focus, you say. Chance would be a fine thing.

But I make a bloody good coffee and walnut cake.[1]

***

---

1 Reekie, Jennie. (1985) *The Little Coffee Book.*

THE JOURNEY

"Encounters with fellow men provide the human mind with invaluable insight" Montaigne

June 1996

Guines

This is the real stuff. We're here, day one, me and the bike, in one of the worst campsites I've ever been in. I'm the only one here. There are caravans but no campers. But there's little point in dwelling on this when there are more serious issues to consider.

I'm supposed to be depressed, but not tonight. It could be the pills addling my brain, but more likely it's Urline. We spoke today. Very formal, no animosity.

I'd better be careful using words like that. I forgot my dictionary so had to buy one at Le Shuttle. I chose the combined dictionary and thesaurus. I debated whether to do without and be self-sufficient but I would be giving up the chance of chance-learning. I have my dictionary, but right now it's too dark to read it.

I had to make a start on my journal before I began my meal. The relationships for tonight are Urline, and my bike. Urline is on hold for the moment but at least the stand-off has been broken and I can discuss my feelings more freely. The bike is different. I've paid it a lot of attention recently and I hope that has put me in good stead. I worried about the condition of the battery at Dover. I had rather neglected that.

But we're here – Guines – 100 miles from home.

The bike seems to be running OK. I ran for about 100 miles without lights. That must have put a better charge in the battery.

I've just cleaned the toilet for the man. You know, the French squat type. It was filthy but there was a brush. I feel quite pleased with myself. It didn't take much effort, and it's fairly presentable now. How's that for self-esteem?

***
Beuzeville

Today I've been rewarded. Here in Beuzeville it's clean and nice and beautiful and cheaper. I should stay two nights.

The point is that I have to attend to bodily functions. I like to leave comfortable and clean, without any itching. So, washing is part of the ritual, and a clean environment is part of that. This is one reason why I don't wish to grow old and be looked after. Nobody will know what I know about myself. This is why good campsites are a prerequisite for a good trip. Mind you, I coped yesterday and left it better than when I arrived.

But the point for today is that when I left Guines, heading west to Brittany was the exact opposite of what I wanted to do.

I want to go to Trieste for a cup of coffee. But Clive Hope believes that if I want to be involved with Partheon then, on the way, I can contact the two French contacts he's had since last year's Royal Show. He's offered 5 per cent commission, with no expenses. It's a fucking insult. It's about as low as you could get without being asked to pay for the privilege of working for him. Yet, I want to be involved. I want to do the job more than anything. I can do this job. But resentment is building up. It's all one way. It's all for his benefit. He can't lose. He's giving nothing in return.

He's exploiting my commitment.

He offered support but nothing happened. He hasn't sent me the pack of brochures he promised. Urline couldn't find the faxes or letters from the two companies so she couldn't give me the telephone numbers. All I had was the man's name and the name of the villages. These could be anywhere in France. International Directory Enquiries couldn't find the numbers for me because I couldn't locate the area. But why me? Why didn't Urline do it? They've got all the information. Perhaps Clive didn't ask her to do it. Maybe these people are no longer in business and here I am, heading for the first visit. It's a long way out of my way for the Italian trip when there's no certainty they exist. Clive and Sunny probably think I'll not bother. This is appalling.

Will I deserve a reward? But life isn't like that, is it? The 'topper' is a good product and Partheon will succeed despite the management. It would do better with me because I'm more proactive on care. I care about the customer and the product, and the way we work together. Relationships need building, need lots of attention. I don't know whether Urline appreciates this; I thought she did. It doesn't extend to me at the moment though.

They use a pasture topper on the sports field at this campsite. A pasture topper is a rotary grass cutter. I can see they do because the topper has left a row of grass to the side of the cut strip. Therefore, it's a belt-driven machine. Partheon's toppers are better than that: they're shaft driven. So, day one, and there's a possibility of there being a market. But do I know the price, the discount, the terms of trade? No. Clive hasn't given these matters any attention. Nor has Sunny – his wife and marketing director – and neither has Urline because, presumably, she's not in the picture. And where are the brochures?

Urline did say she would write and send brochures to the two companies, so my relationship with her is better, isn't it? Is she aware that her letter and my visit give me the resolve to recover a lost position? No contact with the French since December, and it's now June! Do they really want to sell, or is this sales trip a manoeuvre to get rid of me?

The small daughter of the campsite owner has asked me if I want bread and croissant in the morning. Aren't people nice? I said yes. Today's bread was tasteless. So, at Fr3.50 it's worth trying a new baker and throwing the other bread away. My croissant was OK but I may as well try another – so much for the waistline. I didn't eat today until four o'clock but tomorrow, with fresh croissants, I can see it being more like eight o'clock in the morning.

I've only had one cup of coffee today. At £1.50 (*onze francs*) I'm not going to go mad on them. Perhaps I will find something cheaper – like this campsite.

I haven't used my dictionary yet. But I haven't used any long words. I'm not quite into relationships yet. But today, at Guines, I had three people helping me find Trémorel: the shop owner; his assistant, who took me to the town hall; and the guy who worked there. So much for the French not liking the English. My doctor said that. It's all balls. We didn't succeed but I discovered the secret of the postcode: it indicates the area. So I bought a map and traced every likely road until I found Trémorel. I think I treat people nicely – even in a foreign language. I even had four kids, average age seven, waving goodbye to me. It's the bike, you see: it singles you out as a good person. All you've got to do is maintain the image.

It's early. Just now, the owner of the campsite explained the intricacies of a French bottle- opener – the *decapsuler*! We are friends in five minutes.

Does he want a topper?

I had a shower tonight. Got in with all my clothes on, except trousers. That was in order to wash them and put some fresh clothes on. That meant my boxer shorts – trendy gear for me.

But as I sat eating my salami and drinking French *bière blonde*, I noticed a hanging testicle. Not a pretty sight, I thought, and I was moved to cover up despite there being no one else around. But I was struck by the contradictions. It seems that males try to give a testicular outline and bulge with their tight jeans or swimming costumes. Is this the promise of fresh genes and of passions gratified? If not, why do males make such a display? I can't believe that any male display whatsoever can give pleasure, but the suggestion that this might be the case seems to be *la raison d'être* for certain fashions. After all, bums and tight trousers meet the criteria of form as well as function as long as we regard bums as something to hold on to or to gratify sensuous needs rather than something that enables us to walk and stand. These last two sentences have no merit, have they?

***

I could weep at the possibilities. How can a bloke get so wound up? These articles: 'The Strategies that Wal-Mart, Canon, The Limited and Ikea use to outflank competitors'. Well, I do. I've invested US$145 in these Reviews.

Look! Somehow I've got to get alongside somebody who shares these ideas and ambitions. Let's try for some kind of excellence. Just to make things better is something, isn't it?

Let's feed the dream. I can't just die in this hellhole.

Well, it's not really a hellhole: I've got a daughter and a son who I get on with. They're super people.

Decision

I'm reluctant to leave this campsite but I'm also curious about Trémorel. So tomorrow, it's moving on again – the last opportunity to head east, not west. The first decision was probably at Abbeville, when I could turn left for Italy or right for Trémorel. I might be procrastinating until the last minute, of course. The costs since Guines are now quite high, so the cost of getting to Trémorel is now much smaller. And there's the promise of a success behind me instead of ahead of me, constantly niggling.

I'll do it. I need some form of 'success' right now. Despite my feelings that Partheon might be making a fool of me, I'm not going to be able to turn my back on this project. Now that I know where Trémorel is I'll head west, do the job for its intrinsic worth, and feel good.

I wonder if my shirt will be dry. I bought it at Bentalls especially for the trip – long sleeves, thick cotton and absorbent. It's like my David Gower cricket hat: it works.

It rained this morning, which caused me to question my departure. But I needed to make progress, so during a lull in the weather I wiped the tent free of surface moisture, packed, and left. It was cold, unlike yesterday, which was too hot for leathers. But today I wore my pullover. Somewhere near Caen it rained very heavily and continued to do so until about five o'clock. By this time I had wet feet, a wet bum and wet hands. Why can't these manufacturers make this gear waterproof? The wet bum is very disappointing. Bikers always sit in a pool of water when it rains, so the seat of the oversuit has got to be waterproof.

I stopped twice – once for coffee: moderate. But in the café I left a pool of water on the seat and the floor. When I apologised the lady at the counter said it was OK. The French are always friendly – did you hear that? – always friendly.

By this time I had come across the *Auberge de Jeunesse* – the Youth Hostel – so I opted for a dry night at eighty francs. I should have camped and faced the cold and damp but my decision was based on prudence, not macho behaviour.

I think I have a more serious problem. The bike is making serious crackling noises from the drive chain, or power chain. As it's Sunday tomorrow I will have to ride it to destruction and get someone to check it on Monday. Perhaps my 'client' can help me. I'm certain I won't make Italy with this noise, and, unlike Pirsig, I can't contemplate fixing it myself. But there's nothing wrong with delegation to another, is there?

There's a skill and a quality with delegation. I've learnt this because of Clive – he hasn't got the first idea how to delegate. Perhaps this is my chance to demonstrate the techniques. I do it with the Alfa, though this is like selecting a person with requisite skills – those skills that I don't have. Delegation implies a certain amount of skill that is only used in the feedback and monitoring mode.

***

This is Chapter 7.[2] I've skipped Chapter 5 temporarily. Chapter 5 has to be a good piece – to make up for all the rubbish in three and one.

Seven is immediate. Got to address these feelings.

I've got this feeling that women are not understandable – well, at least they cause you to get it wrong and end up in trouble, in love, and out of luck.

Isn't it obvious she fancies me? No. It's stupid. Nothing 'fits'. Wrong age, wrong situation. Wrong. Arrogant.

Babe in arms.

Is it possible to find out what woman is? What, not who? Not why? No. What are women? Why am I not in control? This is not physical. Not physical, like hot and sweaty. More like closeness. More than that – wholeness. Making whole.

See, I've been distracted by her call. I was expected to give up my 'vital' work in order to stay attentive and devoted to her, however discordant with the relative activities. Her need is greater than mine?

***

---

2 I had an agreement with Urline that I would write the odd chapters, and she would write the even.

Rennes

I've been reading David Lodge today and his story has a close resemblance to mine before I left home. My circumstance, now, is much more self-reliant. Once I leave one location, I have no notion of where I shall sleep the coming night, or whom I will meet, or what circumstances I will find myself in. My support system is just me, and a certain amount of insurance in extreme circumstances.

You see, I could have turned left to a campsite just minutes after I had seen the sign for the *Auberge*. My decision to keep to the original decision means that I am dryer and better fed, though much later to bed. But I haven't been able to demonstrate my fortitude in the face of adverse effects of the weather. I am a member of the Youth Hostel Association though, and as the dentist once said, "Why put up with it when you don't have to?" The answer is that I don't know how I would have coped.

What am I going to do with this one-third bottle of wine? I thought it had a cork but it was only a plastic stopper, and I have damaged it. I offered the wine to the girls in the kitchen but they declined. I got a chocolate biscuit in return though. This went with my coffee. I was feeling withdrawal symptoms and, because I had facilities in the Youth Hostel, I bought some coffee.

Now that I drink coffee at the right strength I have the problem in that I can no longer tell that it is coffee. I know it's not anything else, but as for detecting a distinctive coffee flavour – I can't seem do it. I'll sort this out in Italy, if I get there.

Tomorrow I must begin the subject of my journal – relationships. I'll wait and see if a certain person comes to mind.

It's sunny today; chilly at first, but now it's warm

***

Chapter 5. Who is twisting this knife in my gullet? It's her, isn't it? No. It's not. But she's part of the scene. There're too many factors for it to be just her. There's R too – her with the straying hand.

You'd think that at my age all the neurones and synapses would be dulled. No; they're more exposed to the elements – raw and ragged.

Where is the real world? Is it on the production line or in the working man's club? Or is it in the organisation, rubbing up with 'the important' and 'the sure', feeling inadequate and pressured, feeling the need to perform? Should I not market myself just as they market washing-up liquid? I must have one attribute worth having. Or should I be somewhere else – in the sunshine, on the bike, looking forward just ten seconds and no circulating thoughts?

No; we need pangs of regret, the happy times past, the lost opportunities, the opposite of depression – what's the word? Why can I never bring it to mind?

And there's her over there: me Ma, forgetful as hell. Me next? Am I just behind her? Not much time left now. Got to get out, get on, get...

***

Success

I've arrived in Trémorel and found Monsieur Gesret. I met his daughter, who gave me the address of this campsite. It's nice and it's the cheapest yet – Fr27.20.

I thought I would fix the bike – the indicators didn't work. Now I know why. I've lost the relay. I must have forgotten to attach it properly, or it broke the rubber mounting. So, not being in a position to fix that, I thought I'd wash and write a piece of my journal.

I haven't washed because it seemed important to get a few thoughts down in my journal first and see what happened next.

You see, I've reached destination number one and it's Sunday, so Clive's mystery tour didn't hold up. I arrived as the elders were leaving church, and there's a big football competition at the other end of the village. All the shops were open so it wasn't difficult to find Daniel Gesret. He wasn't there but his daughter has invited me back later. So here we are: 14.00 hours, in the tent, contemplating my first meeting.

What shall I tell him about Clive and Partheon? That they're impolite and unprofessional bastards but make a good topper? Perhaps the shadow side of Partheon isn't for this journal. Since they have other characteristics, mostly admirable, I should behave more circumspectly. "Be nice to your enemies; it'll confuse them," said Rosie. (I had met Rosie at the gym when I tried to start a conversation club – to explore the merit of having a leader to allow the quiet to talk and to quieten the noisy?)

I think the problem with the Hopes and Urline is that they're too young – not old enough to say, "I'm sorry you feel like that. What shall we do to make it better?" That's a whole lot better than "So you're saying it's all my fault, are you, Baroux (my French nickname)?" and "You can't blame Partheon for all of this!"

I suppose they'll have an excuse for not giving me an information pack for today.

It's a good job I'm on a bike and camping. Who would expect a super salesman to be such an oddball?

I hope we get on all right. I've not met a French person yet who hasn't been extremely nice to me. So let's wash and go.

***

The Jam!

> *This soup is good. I got the ham bone from Tesco's, free – the tab end of their 'ham off the bone'. So it's this, plus red lentils and cumin and chilli. OK, "So what?" you say. "We all cook brilliant dishes from time to time." Well, it's important to me. Now. It's an island of pleasure – intense pleasure in this sea of depression. I'm happy. What more can a man want? Complete happiness. No: let's be realistic.*

> *No, I'm not being miserable or depressed; I'm telling you the way it is. If you're lucky, that is.*

> *I made jam the other day: THE JAM. It's not only that I made it – you could have made it. Just follow Laurine et al.[3] This*

---

3 Croasdale, Laurine; Jackson, Felicity; LeBlanc, Beverley; (1985) Good Housekeeping.

jam was the result of the fruits in the garden – fruits whose external appearance was green, ugly and forgotten. Quince. Japanese. What emerged was an extraordinary brown-orange translucent jelly with a delicious and delectable flavour. I don't want your admiration; I want you to share it. Isn't that what pleasure is – the sharing of something? A mutual feeling that this something is 'good' – supreme of its kind?

***

Trémorel

Marie-Françoise is the daughter's name. She is studying business in Nantes. The way they do it is by listening to the experience of the chief executives of large and medium-size companies, plus having several periods of internship. She also studied marketing and finance in the US. So, I ought to be able to relate to her. As father spoke no English and I no French, Marie was our interpreter. I think we got on quite well. Father said he was interested in our product and it seems there is a market for it in France, but it will all hinge on the discount. When I pushed for an indication, he spoke of 40 to 45 per cent – that's 20 to 25 per cent for him, and 20 per cent for the dealer.

Obviously that is too much, and he will no doubt accept less. But we have a ball park figure.

Partheon had a partly finished topper in the workshop. It was a four-foot or five-foot machine. This perhaps confirms that the French use such grass cutters; and M. Gesret was interested in a nine-foot topper from Partheon.

Our next step is to demonstrate a topper, and he has invited us to show it on his stand at the SPACE exhibition. I need to be clear about this; I believe it is his stand.

The language could be a problem as Marie Françoise is only available at weekends. We could use the fax machine, of course, but M. Gesret then needs to wait for his daughter to return. I saw the fax from Urline but it was ignored because M. Gesret speaks no English. Never mind: we made progress and wasn't I lucky it was Sunday, when Marie Françoise was home? Father advised us to be careful in the South of France – there is a record of them being bad payers.

It's now six o'clock and I'm about to start on my wine, bread and salami – all from Trémorel. The cheese is from Rennes.

I'm wondering if the crackling and knocking noise from my bike's transmission is to do with a new drive sprocket, a partially worn chain, and a very old rear sprocket. The distance across the seat of the sprocket teeth will have a different diameter and shape to that of the chain link, and the drive sprocket will be different to the rear-driven sprocket, so the links of the chain won't fit either and will be reformed with each revolution of the sprocket. I wonder if an accurate diagnosis fits Pirsig's Quality, or is just doing it the main factor?

The light is fading fast now, and it's almost too late to write. But there is something in me that is compelling me to write, so I thought I would explore this feeling. I'm feeling alone and dependent on my own devices. This is also not a nice place to be, so I want to get away from it. I can put up with the smells from the drains and the poor design, because I can get away in the morning. But this isn't the answer. I'm still me in this world of them. It's a lost cause.

This place is designed to prevent theft: no toilet paper, and lights that go out before you've finished your shower. Is this what humanity deserves? But then I'm only paying twenty-seven francs. Should I be grateful? I'm clean and oiled and presentable. I had my evening repast sitting under the tree, eating a 'forearm' of French loaf, with salami, cheese and wine.

So, what's wrong? It's the same as what has always been wrong. Where is the like-soul with whom to share all this? In this context, 'soul' must mean mental, physical and spiritual. And 'spiritual' must mean the unreason, the philosophical Quality referred to by Pirsig – the euphoria and the despairs that come and go because of life's perturbations. Let's go to bed now and head south in the morning. Into the sun and an even redder nose (the only thing that's really exposed on a motorbike).

***

October 1995

OK. She didn't ring.

She's got other things to do. She has her man. So where do I fit in?

Well, we had a good day yesterday. She did ring. And I rang her.

And...

I...

felt...

her...,

it...,

her.

I can write this because I'm on my own. I don't have to defend my emotions. I may need to explain. Only to me.

I've had a big day, in the sense that I was performing in the presence of people who can affect my life – albeit only in a negative way. If they felt positive about me, it is unlikely that they would tell others about it.

So, I feel under the influence of negative responses. Hence the need for a mate – her.

If I was in a more sober frame of mind I could muscle up two scenarios. I could join my kids but I have no energy. So I would do what 'others' would do.

I'd like to tell you this without interruption. There may be long pauses because I may forget where I'm going – but I'll get there.

There must have been some poet somewhere, sometime – probably in America – who said "Life's a bitch". Life has its upsides, but they're transitory – they don't last forever. You end up with so much regret. Why didn't I spend more time with my kids? I was there. I did play with them, but not enough. They're gone. I can't get them back. That's what I mean by upsides being transitory.

Downsides are different. You know. You've been there. Slightly different – but you're damaged. It maybe heals in time but with scar tissue – still sensitive to the touch.

When I had my difficult period I had been through a long period of normality – just a normal guy. I loved R. I may love her now more than I did then. I can't go back because I don't have that passion, that push in the back – woof, and you're in, driven.

Then the trauma of divorce. How does a normal guy like me end up in the garden, cutting my own throat, and finding peace when I thought I'd managed it? This wasn't a 'damage attack', like Princess Di. I wasn't hurt on the inside. I wanted out.

What's the phrase? I live on borrowed time? Something like that.

Anyway, I got past that, loved some, cried some, wanted my lad back, couldn't think about the future. Just drove on, in the dilemma. Wouldn't someone come and help me? I gave up the future and said I didn't care what happened to me. I would have to cope with it when it came. A lot of that thinking is still there. I'm still irresponsible with regard to it. But, here I am, in my future. And there you are, part of it.

PERTURBATIONS

Oh boy, today!

We – me and the bike – left Trémorel in bright sunshine, bike going well, heading for the Suzuki dealer to fix the indicators and the crackling, knocking chain. Unfortunately the petrol station didn't accept Mastercard. Frizzell had turned me down for Visa, so I had to pay cash. Well, Mondays are days when French bankers and French motorcycle dealers are closed.

Well, so what? I've got credit cards, the bike is going, and life is good. But at Rennes and Angers, damn it, my Eurobank card is not accepted by the technology. I haven't seen a bureau de change, but I do have eighty francs.

Anyway, somewhere in mid-France I stop for coffee and a croissant. That's when I found I had eighty francs. So I bought two croissants. But, would you believe it, the coffee was a dream come true. Unbelievably good. The *Monsieur le Propriétaire* showed me the packet – only for professionals – Jacque something's 'Symphony' coffee. So I had two and that was Fr40.10 (£5.00). So what? That was my breakfast and lunch.

Next came a petrol stop, when neither credit card worked. So the attendant accepted a cheque. Are people here nice? I checked the tyres, oiled the chain, and prepared properly. Pirsig would be proud of my attention to Quality. Then a few spots of rain prompted a full oversuit and a tank bag cover-up. How good was that decision?

It was the heaviest rain I've biked in and I'm pushing on to get to Poitiers to find a bureau de change in order to get some money. If the campsite is more than thirty francs I am in trouble.

Well, trouble comes in funny measures. First the sun came out, and it was beautiful. Then the clutch cable broke. I was fifteen miles from Poitiers. I made it all but about a mile when I had to stop at the traffic lights. I couldn't start again.

So I walked to a repair and paint shop that was called a 'garage'. The boss couldn't speak a word of English but he let me use the phone. But then! "Oh, not more angst, today of all days." I muttered. I discovered I hadn't got any breakdown insurance! It was only personal insurance.

So. Broken down, no money, no insurance. My hope was that CSMA could help – which they did: they made contact with a bike shop – and that, being a biker, my credentials were good.

After about fifteen minutes I decided to walk back to my bike, get my French book, and spend the time usefully. But just as I was about to walk away from the bike Claude rolled up with about three words of English, one of which was 'shit'.

His diagnosis – and this will interest Pirsig and the Anglo-Saxon world – was that he couldn't fix the bike today, but was OK for tomorrow afternoon.

Then something very interesting happened – which is why you've had to read rather a lengthy preamble. Let's not call it luck or skill, but just a different kind of quality to that described by that Pirsig, although of the same genera.

Claude looked at the loose cable. I pointed to the other end and he said, "No problem." Those are his other two words. He then began to take the casing off and I didn't have sufficient French to tell him to stop wasting his time. The crash bar has to come off as well, damn it.

He's mad – too quick by half – but once the casing was off we found it was not the cable that was broken; it was the piece that enables the pulled cable to operate the screw that operates the clutch push rod. Now this piece of equipment is like a small metal box, into which the cable slots. This box had broken in half. This box is very close to the chain and drive sprocket!! Was this the knocking noise I could hear? Let it be – and cure two problems in one.

Claude then proceeded to attach a piece of wire to the clutch cable – the half-box – saying to me, "It is possible, yes?"

OK, he knew seven words. I'm not sure that I know those words in French. Why should he know the English? It smacks of a combination of confidence and Sod's law.

His idea and my idea of fixing the problems were different – but fix them he did. So, in half an hour I was running again.

He then led me to this campsite – the municipal campsite – and Claude has fixed up for his friend at Motostart to fix my bike tomorrow. Not only that, my Anglo-Saxon Europhobes, he's arranged for the campsite manager to ring the workshop for me in the morning.

And no, it's not finished! I was booking in and I said to the manager, "*L'argent?*" He said the French equivalent of "no problem". He then took twenty francs off me, which I thought was a deposit. Then he gave Fr8.45 back and I got on a mathematical muddle, I thought I'd paid Fr115.50. But it wasn't Fr115.50, was it? It was Fr11.55 – less than £1.50 a day!

As Alec in Cyprus would say, "Tell me about it, will yer?"

So here I am: washed, clean, washed shirt and undies, thinking about today. And remember, I've got a 'forearm' of French bread left – a bit stale, but so what? – one third a bottle of wine, and two slices of salami. It'll do, won't it?

November 1995

Contemplation

I have switched the radio off in order to think. I have not done that for a long time – perhaps never before. All the time, I have filled my empty spaces with action or sound – never just me. Even now, I'm writing – but I don't know whether it's the same thing as talking. How do you know what you think, what your opinion is, until you've heard yourself say it?

I don't think writing is the same. It's too slow. I can't keep up with my thoughts so I don't have any (to speak of). That's a joke, by the way!

Speaking is different because it's instantaneous – talking to yourself, I mean – the inner thoughts. There's a conversation going on. It's experimental. You're just trying it out before committing yourself to sound.

Writing has this quality of completeness. There's a thought – now words on a page. Some of it even makes sense. Clever, really, when you think about the grammar and also the progression of ideas. Whether you like them or not, there is a coherent flow. Something is sorting it out.

Anyway, the thought... the silence... the communication. It's to you. You know that, don't you? You're special. I think it's you that brings it about. I need an audience. This audience is restraining. Gives the flow of ideas some point, whatever that means – an objective. The point is to bring you close.

***

Poitiers

Laurence arrived around ten to pick up my bike. He had spent a year in Cannock, near Birmingham, so his English is quite good. He took me to the workshop and I spent the next five hours walking around Poitiers. So my holiday was turning into something of a hiking trip too.

Had another good cup of coffee; does it matter if I don't go to Trieste? The Italians don't drink their coffee in such large volumes – *le grand café*.

How could I afford it, you ask? Well, I went to the bank with my traveller's cheques, and they told me they didn't deal with such things. "Try our branch in the town." But, on leaving, I tried my Eurocard in the machine. Now I was rich again, still having this mixed bag of luck.

After five hours of walking, I thought it was enough. However, I needed a supermarket. I needed toilet paper and soap and bottle-openers and bottles of beer. Supermarkets are not the kind of place to visit on foot. I was directed to one but the guy who told me didn't realise I was walking. That was a fruitless trip. I never found it.

There's a young couple at this campsite and she has a very pronounced bum – the next size up from delectable. He doesn't appear to have one. His trousers droop at the back. I thought ladies liked men with bums. Perhaps MacWilson was right: "It takes a lean dog for a bitch!"

Now, next pitch but one is a caravan with an attractive lady in it. She's walked past a few times now. The last time was to shower – in the men's room!

Good job I cleaned it up. I'm operating my two-flannel system. One is for me and the other is for cleaning up, standing on, and doing my bike. To clean the bike flannel I use it on me, and the shower floor. I hope she noticed. She's walking round again – with her poodle. She's ignoring me. Bet she doesn't like bikes.

This is an afternoon writing session. I think I'm at the limits of my intelligence, I'm not sure. I ought to be writing something profound – my writing is too descriptive, isn't it? When I read something deep when I was working, the brain used to 'ache'. This happened when I first started my degree too. But after a time it wore off and I could read more easily and with no ache. I'm sure the brain is a muscle, and needs exercising. I don't know whether I'm not working it hard enough or whether it's in good condition. It doesn't ache now! It might be a mite pickled in alcohol and caffeine.

I haven't had an important thought today. Perhaps the various perturbations that are going on are filling up my mind. Perhaps I need a period of solitude. On the other hand I might need stimulation by others – real, or in prose. Perhaps it's time to dip into Pirsig.

***

This is the first occasion when I have, metaphorically speaking, started out with a blank sheet of paper. It's not been a good week so far. I expect things to pick up, but hopefully the happenings will have some association with work, not people. Women, I mean. But you might construe alliteration as spurious.

I've got no future. I could pull myself together and go and learn French or history. Egan speaks of people being mired in their personal problems – unable to get out because they cannot envision or conceptualise a state of affairs where they are different to what they are now.

I cannot see me being 'coupled' happily again. I am now friendly with more blokes than women. There's no commitment with blokes. George Eliot supposed that this condition could be established with women – but the condition of no passion or emotion to give or accept is difficult to experience. Women are a rare experience anyway without finding that cuddling up in bed is a good place for a chat. That's exceptional.

You can't do that with a bloke.
There's no logical reason to expect a happy situation to materialise in the future. There might be a reason based on making an effort some time in the future. I could do that now. I'm working at finding the energy for that – going out at night. Pubs? Diners?

***

I have a problem. Laurence says the bike might be ready on Sunday morning. That's two and a bit days away. And I've got a blister on my foot and my groin is beginning to hurt.

What am I going to do for two days? There is a certain routine that I like: coffee and croissant around ten or eleven in the morning. But I need to find useful activity. I have found most of the functional centres: post office, supermarket, choice of coffee and bread shops. I even know where to get my shoes repaired. So the walks are getting shorter because I know where I'm going, and this saves the blister and the groin, and also allows my shoes to last.

Money is also a problem – these credit cards aren't working. Is this an international problem, or just the way I keep them?

Having said all that I dip into Pirsig, and I had a shot at Gaarder (*Sophie's World*).

Many of my better thoughts occur to me when I'm either walking or eating. On neither occasion can I write. Pirsig seems to arrive at a place, and from that can relate to two or three connected events. Did he stop the cycle and write it all down? Or did he write it all down and imagine he was on a journey?

He said his journey is based on actual occurrences. Now I can believe that; I seem to need occurrences too. That's why two days restricted to walking range could be short on occurrences. Perhaps not – *ne peut-etre!*

Pirsig seems to want to argue that reason is not enough, or is even inhibiting. A job well done, the epitome, no, the essence of Quality, is his notion of what life should be about – not just the execution of reason if A then B, but doing A to the highest standard using one's intuition, one's instinct, as well. As Pirsig stated: "The place to improve the world is first in one's own heart and head and hands, and then work outward from there."

Gaarder explains that the Greek philosophers began with questions. He knows some of their conclusions – Aristotle wrote them down. But we don't know what questions were asked.

I think I find the question the more alluring. Good execution must come from good analysis in the first place. But I'm not entirely satisfied with that. That's because execution can come in two forms (let's forget the substandard): first, the *satisfactory* quality where, or when, it is fitted to the purpose – that is, it doesn't exceed the purpose. The second form is where a person does the job to the highest possible standard, and it becomes an art and a joy of itself.

I think I have an understanding of this. I have attempted to achieve an as high as possible standard in all that I do. This was often criticised in my civil service career. But it seemed to me that by stretching to achieve the higher standard, even more was learnt.

Right now my thoughts are returning to Partheon and how badly I have been treated. I don't think I can possibly get back into the former situation. If they consider the offer of 5 per cent commission on sales sufficient for the work that is needed to secure a market in France, they are misleading themselves and they are abusing me. Having a twelve-year-old bike partially worn out is symptomatic of not having sufficient money to maintain my assets. I wonder if they'll ask me how I have got on. By 'they' I mean all three – Clive, Sunny and Urline. I am going to try and restore the position but I fear that I shall have no option but to leave them. I regard this as a personal tragedy to have these people turn their backs on me and remove their friendship. What thought processes can bring such a thing about?

***

What would it be like to write when there is no urge to put pressing thoughts to paper? 'Start' is the general advice, and let creativity take over.

Well, the subject for today is 'How do you spend the rest of your life?' All other things being equal, is it possible to reach a stage when striving for fulfilment has to give way to experiencing life? I would have said 'happiness', but that is too ambitious.

***

One of the problems with a journal is that it is natural to make it chronological. This one has been so far. Well, it would be. I don't have a word processor and I begin each section where I left off.

You see, I have had 'occurrences' today. I have also spoken to Partheon.

All my inner conversations were with Urline, and I was going to refuse to speak to Clive. But when I rang, Clive answered, so that blew all those plans. I asked if they had sent the brochures to the contacts. This really was an excuse for ringing. But, can you believe it: Urline had written but not sent brochures. These are the people who are making judgements about me.

C'est la vie!

I also rang my credit card bank to tell them my credit cards were not working. They told me that because the French had introduced a 'chip' into their cards, UK cards can no longer be read. Never mind 'mad cow disease'; when are they going to sort this form of co-operation out?

My next occurrence was a visit to see Laurence at the bike shop. He tells me the bike will be fixed for tomorrow afternoon – Friday. That's good, isn't it? But Laurence has this unemotional manner of speaking, so when he told me yesterday, in about the same tone, that the bike wouldn't be ready till Saturday, I didn't believe him. It's strange, that: the French usually speak with inflection in their voice, which gives 'feeling' to what they say. I wonder if English **syllabification** prevents this.

I then visited 'my bar' for the second day running. It must be the best in Poitiers. I know they charge a bit more – Fr19.50 for coffee and a croissant – but I can watch everybody walk by, and 51 per cent are female. I tried to read Gaarder, but not very successfully. So what? This is what drinking coffee in France is all about – a good location with interesting views. Even the people in the café are interesting, and well beautiful too. I really like France. The coffee is good – not as good as 'north of Angers', but better than I can make. So I have been a bit extravagant today. 'My' coffee cost £2.50 (Fr19.50), and then I bought another *demi* for six francs, and then, because I thought I deserved it, I bought a beer at the Café de Paris – a local bar at a crossroads en route to the campsite. I've been before; the coffee is good, but tonight I found out what a *croque-monsieur* is: a toasted ham and cheese sandwich.

***

*"I want to hear that you've done it the next time that we meet,"
she said.*

*Well, if I really had to make a decision like that, it would drive
me right into that corner that I studiously avoid. It's the bloody
trade-off all the time – the zero-sum game. When the decision is
important, when it means heading off in a particular direction,
it also means giving up that part of life that we also value.*

*But I like meeting you too, don't I?
Just supposing I do meet a darling of a girl in furs who's
got nothing better to do than dote on me! No: that's stupid,
too trivial a comment. She will come with a burden too. Is it
possible to reach this age and not be troubled with thoughts
that nothing is for ever?*

*Do I have to be serious about this – to analyse personal decision
making? Is there a natural life to relationships when its end
comes and goes with nobody noticing? Or is there an inertia
which keeps you locked into the current situation? More often,
I think it is the latter. Whilst Bob Hoskins, or BT, says "It's
good to talk", there is a waning and waxing of interest and
commitment in giving another your attention. Consequently,
it's necessary to end it sometime, but the initiative is more
often taken by the other person – to avoid hurt.*

*Given that no action is taken if hurt is a probability, then
self-inflicted hurt is likely to follow the same course. Hence,
we are going to settle for the status quo most often. Dynamic
conservatism is difficult to overcome!*

*The risks involved in being adventurous – heading into the
unknown – are coupled with the realisation that life is not
fair and it doesn't favour the brave. If the venture fails, then
neither fairness nor bravery have been a saving grace. It's not
like rolling dice. Dice do not have memory. If they did they*

would not roll true; they would have a bias and would not give you a straight outcome.

The argument that the present is not lost because it is possible to return has a slight flaw. The decision involves weighing the future possibility against the present. It implies movement from one to the other, with memory attached. You only contemplate letting go because you can't have both. You're going to lose one, and that's the one you know.

I am wondering if it would be good policy to tell her how I feel. I had the thought that it would be easier to tell her and walk away, than to just walk away.

Why walk away? Well, there's no future for our relationship. Rather than create a complex situation where feelings are transmitted and, let's say, understood; then transmuted – rescinded – having taken root; what seems to be important is for us to communicate our feelings. This is what makes us human beings civilised human beings: the fear of hurting others, dissimulation unconscious.

This was supposed to be a happy piece, straight from the happy button!

***

I haven't had the chance to tell you: French behaviour when telephoning is odd. Last night the nearby telephone was occupied for two to three hours. Outside the booths there are queues, and a seemingly constant flow of people. I thought I could beat the system, so walked for ten minutes to a couple of booths that I thought would be empty. I waited for fifteen minutes there too, only to find that the lines to the UK were blocked. So, I had to walk back again.

When I got back, the phone box was empty but the lines were still blocked, but I got through on the fourth try by operating the 'persistent' regime. I was trying to check whether my mother could lock the back door now that the double glazing had been fitted. She said she couldn't. So, I sent her back to try it with the door handle 'up'. She was gone a long time, but eventually came back to say she couldn't find her keys. So, what the hell was she doing the first time! She seems to be happy with the double-glazing, so that's good. It'll save me a lot of work. Perhaps we can make her flat nice in other ways too.

I rang Trixie tonight but she wasn't in. So, I rang Natalie. I was going to ring Urline first but thought I better hadn't. 'People' might question my priorities. By 'people' I think I mean R. I know that I have a voice at my shoulder constantly questioning my motives, but I'm pretty sure R had the edge on this occasion.

Natalie sounded pleased to hear from me, which was good. I don't know why I wanted to ring her but there is a shortage of people to talk to here – those who can speak English, anyway.

Perfection

Intimacy and communication are inextricably connected.
When we speak of communication, we mean more than just
the ability to discuss problems and resolve conflicts. We mean
communication for its own sake: the pleasure of being in
each other's company, the excitement of conversation, the
exchange of touches and smiles, the loving silences. Through
communication we disclose who we are, and from this
self-disclosure intimacy grows.

Strong and DeVault 1992

I bought a bottle-opener yesterday – a *decapsuler*. This opener has the capacity of putting the cap back on again. Now the number of times you find it necessary to recap a bottle is minuscule, but this strikes me as one of those Quality features Pirsig would appreciate: beyond reason but clever and skilful. I bought a bottle of beer tonight in order to try the opener but I haven't done it. I had too much wine and I had had a beer *pression* at the Café de Paris before I came 'home'.

You might not regard these as 'relationships', but they are to me. It's an attitude towards life that impinges upon people.

One of the more important relationships when I go on holiday is the style and cleanliness of the toilets. The toilets at this site are the continental squat type. (I understand that they are Turkish.) I think I prefer these, but having walked for five or six hours today the last thing I felt like doing was squatting on my hunkers. I think the main point – if you don't mind me discussing it – is that the act is successful and clean. There must be something physiologically correct about the posture. I don't know why they are going out of fashion. It can only be that the act of standing up from a squat position without aid from the arms must be difficult for many people.

Having done flannels, soap, bottle-openers and squat toilets, there must be the opportunity now to move on to higher things.

Why do the couple next door always go to the ablutions together? She's watching him shave! And why don't they bother whether it's male or female?

***

Well, she rang. Isn't that good?

We've discussed that before, so I won't bore you again. What is this happiness? What does it mean? How does it affect us? Doesn't it switch our attention from the self to the life outside our self? It sets us free to experience other possibilities in life. If, at least, one person believes in us then we can meet others on equal terms and perform more nearly to our current potential. Maybe experience a chance happening that takes us beyond our ability and into a new learning situation. Jargon? Well, how would you say it?

What's important is the reassurance that gives us belief in our abilities. Searching for people to share our enthusiasms. This is not competitive – it's 'combining', a meeting of minds. This seems to happen when we hear people on the radio but it's rare in a person-to-person meeting. Is this because the 'real' person has idiosyncrasies that offset their talents and so diminish our admiration to 'mere' respect for their performance?! Madonna is like this: she has given a performance that we can all admire. We don't need to approve of her values or her choice of subject, but we can be enthralled by the combination of talents that is responsible for the Madonna-performance in its entirety.

I've just listened to Freddie Mercury, and now to Paul Simon. I wondered if they were profound enough, so I picked out Rupert Brown's Group Processes. *I didn't really have the choice, did I? I needed to experience Mercury and Simon and I needed the explanation of Brown too – that's if it can be explained.*

It does matter, to some extent, if he can't explain it, but only in that we haven't reached the ultimate truth. What we have is a better understanding, a little bit nearer the truth. And that's satisfying.

I mustn't paraphrase any more, otherwise I shall only summarise the book.

***

I seem to be developing relationships with a number of people, largely because I don't speak the language. There's Laurence at the bike shop, the waiter at the coffee bar, the couple at the local small supermarket, the assistants at the delicatessen in each supermarket, and the manager of this campsite – a whole lot who seem to be eager to help me. The ones who have been doubtful are the lady in the *office de touriste*, who was not sympathetic to my credit card problem; and the checkout assistant at the supermarket, when I hadn't weighed my fruit and my credit cards didn't work. I had a big queue behind me so I wasn't popular even though I had a funny hat on.

Tomorrow is a big day. My street cred should be restored when I get my bike back. It raises you above the ordinary when you've got a bike. You're suddenly a member of a select group. I'm looking forward to that.

I've made a mistake with these jeans. They're too tight. I thought they might be better for the bike but they're only for posing in. I'm at the Café de Paris for my coffee and croissant – sixteen francs. Their coffee has very little *crema*– the foam on top of espresso – *and* now I'm into it, the coffee could be stronger. I'm becoming a connoisseur now: I can tell the difference between this coffee and that at Le Gambetta bar in the centre of town. Instead of admiring the street walkers there – the ladies in their French black-style dress – I have a girl in front of me taking lettuce out of a plastic bag, tearing it with her hands, and placing it on a plate. There are twelve plates – four of them slightly smaller than the others. Now grated carrot, chopped ham, then eggs, and what looks like cheese.

Did I say I need a plan? I remember having one of these inner conversations with you, suggesting that for 'anti-plan' man to express such a need was perverse. I think I concluded that a wait-and-see incremental policy was in order because I couldn't plan without resources or knowledge – like a bike and knowing when it would be ready.

***

Let's return to 'her'. Does she materially influence my future behaviour? I can certainly find myself attracted to places within her orbit. This precludes entering into another orbit and finding new relationships. The pull of a new relationship is quite powerful, and so it's a mitigating factor in 'nesting' in a known and accepting orbit. Is this the difference between men and women?

It would confuse desire to combine two orbits in order to inhabit both at the same time. To inhabit both orbits alternately would eventually end in neither orbit being hospitable, wouldn't it? Insufficient input of energy would result in a decrease in the inclination to stay in place and to increase the inclination to find attentive relationships in other areas. Orbits could have more than one energy source, and, perhaps support a thesis that to properly maintain a relationship it is necessary to provide energy from an external source. To concentrate energy on a single interest might bring it to a higher state of activity.

I like the last paragraph. It tends to confirm Malcolm Bradbury's latter-day approach of starting to write and finding word associations in order to develop the story. Domain might have been a better analogy than orbit, though.

***

Hanging about in Poitiers has been quite good. Time has passed. I've been shopping, window shopping, and drunk beer and coffee. I've read a little and written a little. I could have done more reading so I wasn't short of things to do. The lass at the counter preparing a salad has put tomatoes on now and I'm wondering if the piece that fell on the floor would have been rejected had I not been here. She checked my observation.

I'm still short on the learned discourse in this journal though. I see that David Lodge has got into the divorce from his wife; and a dirty weekend away with his friend Amy and description of how she got rid of floating turds in the toilet in their scrubby hotel in Tenerife. Now I could get into this because of my 'occurrence' in the toilet this morning. Whilst it might be of passing interest what people do in their most private moments, I'm not sure that it is 'prose'. On the other hand, for me, it influences a large part of my life and my view regarding the future.

You see, the need to go to the toilet is frequently signalled by 'itching'. If that cannot be resolved then washing is a good cure. What nursing home, when you're ninety-two, can be sensitive to these things? Also, there are protuberances that are either piles or intestine that I need to push back, and quite often the clean-up operation is not quite as effective as I would like. In strange places I spit on the paper, and usually that works. At home I can wash, and that's better. Now all this means that I need access to facilities. It is better if I'm at home and in control. To be in some dodgy French campsite or in some ill-kept pub in Chipping Sodbury makes me a home-loving boy with no great desire to get old and decrepit. So, having set such parameters, the plan is to find a decent *sanitaire* in the Massif Central by Saturday night.

I've just read *Dover Beach* by Matthew Arnold. Rosie gave it to me. She said 'it' and 'he' were pessimistic about life. I wonder. I'm not pessimistic right now. Apart from Clive Hope and Sunny, I find most people extraordinarily courteous and helpful, particularly in France. This could be whilst I'm of sound mind and body – my mother's condition is of concern. That's why I moved in with her. Perhaps, when I'm 'past it', I have to accept that there is "neither joy, nor love, nor light". Well, there is something. The girl doing the food smiles at me. She doesn't have to do that. So whilst there is some 'communality' we are in a better position to protect ourselves in situations than "where ignorant armies clash by night!"

Rosie gave me a notebook – an 'ideas' notebook. I have a number of ideas which I would like to capture in writing, but they elude me when the time to write comes.

***

Dear Baroux,

Thanks for the letter; it was good to hear from you. Our relationship has not changed. You are you and I am me. We are the same people, just farther apart. I feel for you and the situation in which you find yourself. Life can be unkind, unjust and unfair, especially to those who have principles and beliefs. Clive (and Sunny) will go far. He is a capitalist; an opportunist. He is extremely ambitious, determined to succeed. The drive to win is very strong in him. He does not have your sensitivity, integrity, or belief in truth and need to stand up for fair play, socialism, or whatever else you care to call it. Unless you have money the latter will not help you to succeed in any business set-up. It is always the ruthless, the unimaginative, the single minded who end up with money and power. So people like you and me either change, or end up with nothing. That is the plain undisguised truth of life as I see it!!

Of course we may not strive for that, but if not we cannot have it both ways; we cannot envy the buggers who have it but despise the methods they use to get it, can we? I am smug in the belief that what I try to do in life is fair. I don't manipulate people; I don't tread on people. I have diplomacy and tact; I try to please, to not be unkind, to live by a code of mutual respect and trust, but this is no good. I get trodden on, used, taken for granted, and am left with feelings of resentment, bitterness and despair, which can't be good, can it? I've got to learn to know what I want, and take it. The only time that I have done this was when I met Bloke, and just look at the pain I have suffered ever since. It is despicable and cowardly. I have to be braver. If I lack morality I have to learn to not give a damn. If I give a damn I must not be immoral – a paradox. Life is full of them. You spoke of male and female relationships. I don't feel equipped to comment, really. Sometimes I feel that I have a power that is startling, that comes from being female. I subdue it because I'm not sure how to control it. Men find me attractive, which surprises me, but then I realise that femininity is an enigma to men. A smile, a look, a platitude, a sensitive ear, and men are lost. I have no wish to manipulate this. I am probably maligning and simplifying male feelings by saying all of this, and it isn't meant to insult or hurt. It is very flattering to be desired. Another problem is the other woman. I don't feel comfortable acting the 'femme fatale' because other women don't like you if you do. Maybe I should think: "Who cares? – this is my life and I'll use my femininity to get what I want." I just need not to have a conscience about it. But if you are talking about friendship – as in you and me – it is good to have someone who cares about you; as you once said, "to know that someone is on your side". I'm glad you are part of my life, and look forward to hearing from you, especially your letters. The written word is much more profound and uninhibited. Also, I am learning to decipher your writing. I hope your interview turns out to be a success. You certainly deserve it; it could open up a whole new source of inspiration and joy. I do hope so.

As to your remarks about your family, I look forward to the day when maybe I will feel needed and appreciated again. I find it hard to earn respect: they make me act from a defensive position, and somehow it lacks clout. Bloke says I have to stand up for myself and not let them dominate me. He says I run around after them too much. But when you live miles from their friends and it was the school of your choice, somehow you feel responsible for allowing them to just be young and free. If that's the case I suppose I shouldn't complain when they take me for granted – I can't have it both ways. Anyway, I've whinged for long enough. Did you watch Wuthering Heights over Easter? Beautiful acting by Olivier but it was only half the story.
Be in touch soon; keep writing.
Love, Urline

***

To live only for some future good is shallow. It's the sides of the mountain which sustains life, not the top. Here's where things grow. Robert Pirsig

Family

David Lodge goes on about Kierkegaard and 'repetition'. He interprets this as a satisfying part of life when less talking is needed and people develop habits that are in accord with one another. I might understand this but I don't agree. What seems more important is to have a stimulus (from an external source?) which two people can share, to feel a mutual pleasure, which, in turn, compounds the pleasure. There is also a sense of security in adverse circumstances. I'm thinking of R here. She was good in adverse circumstances – she had faith in me and could tolerate things being bad. Where we had problems was sharing some of the so-called pleasures. She could spoil a good film by objecting to sex in the story, for example, when, of course, I got a bit more pleasure from the sight of a bare buttock, or boob or two. Nor do I mind people making love. I can share that emotion when it is well portrayed.

I've just rung Trixie. She was out. R was engaged. Charlie (my son) I spoke to for about twenty minutes. It was good to tell him what I was up to.

I almost rang Urline but backed off at the last moment. I had no intention of speaking to her. I was going to let the phone ring once and then put it down. Childish really, but it is symptomatic of still liking her a great deal. I am still very upset about the whole Partheon attitude, but, there we are. Let's put it down to adolescence. I heard a biannual reunion broadcast recently by ex-students of the all-women's Smith University in the USA. One woman made the point that we should give up seeking perfection. I think that applies more to Partheon than me; they are the losers by maintaining their attitude. If they included others with different values – a dissonance – then not only would we have someone working engaged with the French market, but Partheon would have a greater probability of achieving it. Now I am very reluctant to tell them anything, even the telephone numbers. I have found the potential buyers. I know where they are, and it's all because I am who I am. I persist and I find things out. They need me, but they think in simpler terms. I have another perspective, which means they think they can do without me. Well, in two days I have done more than they have done in six months. It's cost me money and time. Whilst I can be benevolent, they must treat me as an equal, not as a bloody peasant who is just around to do their inadequate bidding – and that goes for Urline too.

My relationship with Charlie and Trixie is different. It's much more serene and trusting but not as close as the Partheon relationship. I believe that this is because with kindred there's a tendency to withhold the more basic feelings, for example, me telling Charlie that I sat in a café watching the girls go by. This isn't what you tell your son. I did but it doesn't feel quite right and does not give the same sense of comradeship.

Rejection

Relationships with Women, Relationships with Blokes

This is difficult to discuss because the feeling a person has for another changes daily, if not continuously.

I was upset today because she was not available to me, either at the time or in the future. Are we bound to feel hurt when another whom we feel very attracted to and fond of cannot respond to those feelings? These feelings can best be described as affections. Another description might be love, but this is a difficult emotion to identify. Perhaps this shouldn't be so when it should be quite normal and acceptable to love more than one person, but in so doing, suffer feelings of deprivation if that love is understandably denied.

These feelings of rejection give rise to strategies that might enable us to restore an equilibrium, and our esteem. To somehow come to terms with the loss of an opportunity to have someone love us – to restore our self-regard. Esteem, I believe, is a belief in our ability; self-regard is a comfortable feeling that, despite our inadequacies, somebody not only has regard, but loves us.

What is the value of describing this situation?

It so happens that this is a relationship between a man and a woman. Can you recall such a situation between two men? Or two women? Perhaps more likely with two women, as my perception is that there is a much more emotional relationship when a female is involved than when there are two males.

Men, perhaps, have a much more secure relationship, or perhaps the male is less dependent on another male for his self-regard. His self-esteem is perhaps dependent on those males and females who only observe the superficial performance. If this is true, how do we explain the satisfaction, the joy, that is experienced when we contact another female after a period of a year or more, and that female is able to express a genuine pleasure in making contact? Isn't that a secure relationship?

Males are casual, bordering on indifferent, if another male should renew the contact. There might be some pleasure when each regards the other as a nice person. George Eliot observed that the best form of companionship is experienced when friendship exists between males and females that have no passion to express or receive. This now seems erroneous when the major difference between a male-female and a single-sex relationship, is that men and women conceive more readily of going to bed with each other than when they are in a single-sex relationship.

Irrespective of these sensual feelings, the relationship between men seems subordinate to a relationship between a man and a woman. At bottom, it is the mitigation of loneliness that is a major benefit of a relationship. It is relationships with members of the opposite sex that build internal satisfactions and a sense of well-being.

Male-male relationships are stimulating from two viewpoints. First, males are competitive where there's a need to have more or better ideas than the other. Second, there is a tendency to dwell more on objective than subjective matters.

These, then, leave the male-female relationship to deal more in the 'soft' emotional issues of which human beings, particularly males, have a great need.

Within these generalisations each relationship has its specific characteristics. Perhaps we could increase our understanding of this by reference to the characteristics required for therapy – genuineness, empathy, and caring.

Not all people have all these characteristics but will have some, to a greater or lesser degree. Each will have its attraction and its beneficial effect for particular individuals. So, different friends provide different things, maybe. The significant relationship is where an individual is able to provide some disparity but which has, in addition, the indefinable chemistry.

***

A Ploy

I think I'll buy Laurence a bottle of wine for his courteousness. I wouldn't like this transaction treated in the ordinary way. I think he has been very good with me and I appreciate it. It's bedtime and yoghurt time now: 9.45 – and still daylight!

I will be up at six thirty to attend to my toilet, preparing to have the bike back. I forgot to tell you. The part didn't arrive today, so, no bike.

I had a lot of arguments with First Direct today. They hadn't heard of the absent chip in the English credit cards. They even said my ordinary debit card would work. I said, fibbing, I'd tried it once but it didn't work. Ha! it has today. I suppose I had prejudged it. Tomorrow I need seven to eight hundred francs for my bike. We shall see.

I wish I was over this bloody French cold. It's now making my nose sore as well as causing dirty handkerchiefs. I've also broken a tooth. This is sodding ageing. I must make the most of this trip.

Some Germans arrived at the campsite and not one of them made any attempt at a greeting. Most French do. Is this German arrogance or reserve?

I'm in 'my' location again, observing the passers-by and trying to write. I think there are more visitors today. It's Saturday. People are less well dressed. It seems in France you can buy your croissant next door and eat it in the café. Do you think I should have started another paragraph to change the subject like that? I think not. They may be disconnected thoughts but they result from immediate events. There are some very nice fashions about – all women, of course. I can't think what men might do. That's very interesting: I've just seen a man carrying a baby in a carrier on his back, and the carrier had a sunshade. I've just finished my second *grand café*. Two seems to be the saturation point. I'm ready for the day now.

I'm committing myself to a plan. I rang Mondial Assistance today to find out if they could obtain – nearly said "source"! – an indicator unit from England and deliver it to an agreed location. Suzuki France don't have one. It seems I have agreed to go to Marseilles airport to pick it up. I explained to Sophia that I was on my way to Trieste for a cup of coffee, which seemed to amuse her.

This is a ploy I use, isn't it? in my relationship building. There's an assumption that I can go beyond the formal, and be informally interesting. R might argue that it's insincere and manipulative. But I feel that I have an ability to communicate at the friendly level, and that causes people to be more willing to be friendly to me. It is better for both of us.

It's not only words, because I think the fact that I have found the French more friendly is because I have a detectable attitude of friendliness. In England this effect is countered by being direct, which can be interpreted as discourteous. There is a degree of openness, or rather directness, which many English people find disconcerting. In France, of course, I do not have the language to be anything other than direct. But the fact that I can ask at the post office where Pennautier is and receive a lot of help leads me to believe that the French are naturally friendly. It was the same at the paper shop when I needed a map in order to locate Pennautier.

***

Never read what you've written when you have the urge to write. Corrections can be made any time. Capturing the feelings is a matter of timing – and once lost, those that replace them lack passion.

I watched the clock go round – as you do when 'she' might ring and you are in total despair – to the point when the moment was fast approaching when 'accepting' the situation was your hole in the corner.
Let's try writing it down. But curiosity about our 'relationship' tempted me, and I found alterations to do.

So now, after she's rung, the emotions calmer, what sort of appeal can this writing possibly have? There's no passion in analysis.

What have I said that I regret? Does it matter? I can be active tomorrow. Leave the bed. Face the world. Laugh. Be strong. Well, pretend a bit – just a little self-deception – something that'll pull the birds, given the chance.

Businesses need women. Groups need women. 'Can do' is induced.

If this is anything like right, why is it not permanently locked in? Wouldn't success be more assured? Does the opposite make the group vulnerable? If we have a part of the brain that can be triggered, then it is a weak point too. Maybe it helps in the sexual selection such that well-formed groups are more creative and survive better.

This narrow boundary between too much and too little love is difficult to manage. It is leading to upset and embarrassment each time chance situations give rise to acts of rejection or too close an attachment.

I find it interesting that following the previous discussion on emotions being a factor in group selection, the article in the Financial Times series 'Mastering Management' on personality and performance hints at the same thing.

It discusses the 'chemistry' that influences relationships between people, which manifests itself as gut feelings, involuntary emotional reactions, sensations of trust and empathy and of revulsion and discomfort. These feelings cause behavioural patterns, which are most likely to surface when there is minimal constraint – as amongst friends – when we have more freedom to act how we want.

We also have a desire to be with each other, to bond and to breed and to accomplish complex and difficult tasks that cannot be achieved alone. This is in addition to the need for us to function autonomously.

To summarise, this material doesn't make for fulfilling or satisfying writing. It is not coming from the heart. But I like to note it, perhaps return to it, in some context.

How is it possible to write with a balance of feeling and intellect, creatively and with relevance? How do you restrain the propensity to produce rubbish? I need to trust my audience but explore the reaches of my experience and hope that I have the ability to be relevant.

Am I hoping to pass on new ideas, or am I just hoping to express old ideas that the audience is pleased to have confirmed? If they are expressions of endearment the recipient might well feel satisfaction, especially when a reaction is not discordant with the felt emotions.

***

To Carcassonne

I've set off again and I'm having a break in a very 'local' café. The coffee has no *crema* and there's more coffee in the cup. There's about ten locals drinking here, and it's about 10.30 a.m. I'm not sure what they will make of this guy in motorcycle gear sat down writing. For some reason, they're all similar: sixty, overweight, weather-beaten – typical French. I can't understand a word they are saying.

I met John last night – an English guy, fifty-eight, from Reading. He has a Honda VHF with panniers. He is a Scouser, and described how Liverpool is what it is because of the people – Irish-Scots. I'll have to research that – why Scots?. He, too, had pressure – he was a chemical engineer who worked for a construction company in the oil business. He didn't talk to the English couple in a caravan next to him. It's to do with bikes.

I'm not well still. I've got this infection of the chest and sinuses and it's not getting better, and my chipped tooth is now cutting my tongue. And the bike is still making that worrying noise at the drive cog end, and it's not the stand knocking – I've tied that up. The clutch has never been better. It's an added pleasure to use it. I bought Laurence a bottle of wine – forty francs. I'm pleased I didn't buy a cheaper one; I think it made a good impression.

The walls in this bar are covered in coloured aluminium foil – red and green. Some customers are drinking white wine with blackcurrant cordial.

I've moved on now to much pleasanter bar – coffee and croissant. The proprietor has lent me some cleaning fluid for my visor. I'm in Seilhac now, about 120 miles south of Poitiers, after four hours of good biking country, a cloudless sky, a cool breeze and virtually no traffic. And here we are, writing again. More description, of course. I thought my title of 'Relationships' was going to provide an ongoing theme, but it hasn't happened. Perhaps without studying psychology there's not a lot to say about relationships. Somehow I have to link it to place and time as well as to occurrences.

I've turned slightly left as I've come down France. I'm headed for Aurilac. I think this is just about on the edge of the Central Massif, and I will look for a campsite there. Tomorrow I shall head south again, to Carcassonne through Rodez. A scenic route is indicated by the map. It seems now that my travelling one hundred miles or so without a stop has been the wrong way to travel. There were a number of medieval castles and bridges, and this appeared to be the route taken by Richard the Lionheart. What is required is more money and a leisurely trip – stopping a while to see what is there and who there is to meet.

I am in the Central Massif now – one of my objectives. I was there with my fifteen year-old son Charlie in 1986 but we didn't stop in the mountains, as far as I can remember. It seemed rather isolated, which could make it more interesting than the lowlands. So I have an expectation. Not of it being grand, as it is, but meeting people and establishing personal relationships. I regret not stopping when I was with Charlie. We passed some sort of hamlet, with people outside, but I needed to find a campsite. It might be like Cumberland, in the Borders, where people are extraordinarily gracious. Gracious was Bill Johnson's word. He worked in the district before Dougy Ironside and me. These were two older colleagues in my early career, and some of the better relationships in my life. Wonder why that is. I knew quite a lot of people who were quite a good deal older than me and R, and I used to get on very well with them. Now it's me that's old, and I have younger friends. It might be to do with communality or co-operation, and the absence of the competition one might face from a peer group. It seems the connection between Aurilac and Bill Johnson is a bit tenuous.

I've read some more David Lodge. He introduced his friends and acquaintances as the storytellers. I've briefly considered this but I'm not keen on writing what would be a fiction. I'm not sure I can see these events I'm experiencing, through other people's eyes. I know I could try. What I feel I want to do is to get out of me what's there. But I'm not doing very well so my tactic is to persist. After all, there have only been limited experiences. Once I'm further south I believe the nature of events will change and be more difficult to deal with.

I was the only one on that campsite – Fr30.50. Now I've only been travelling twenty minutes – 30-m.p.h. corners with *chassée deformée*, followed by some 70- to 80-m.p.h. curves. And the bike? Going like a dream. I've just realised bikes are 'she's – *la moto* – so perhaps 'she' is responding to me looking after her a bit. Did I tell you I washed her with soap and water ? Smells as good as me now. And my hands are a lot cleaner.

Anyway, I've stopped. Maurs looked quite nice but it's too hot to sit in the square. The coffee is not bad but not up to Angers's standard. I'll have to go home that way.

Sublimation

This day has had difficulties for me. I become increasingly despondent as tomorrow draws near. No contact from people who have emotional control over me. I conclude that my involvement in their work and lives is practically nil, and I have to fend for myself in terms of friendship and intellectual stimulus.

Russ Hayton

OK, so what's new? you might ask. Well, it's fairly new to me. If I think in terms of both together, it is wholly new.

I don't feel like growing some more, going through the whole damn process of feeling down and putting a brave face on it and going out and finding some more interests and income. Each time, or this time, it might be the time of discovering the truth of how dispensable I am and how valueless is my ability. This, at a period when I feel I know more and feel that I could make a contribution.

Urline is key to this. She faces almost the same problem but with an added dimension – she must have the money. She also wants involvement and she wants to be wanted. But not by me. The fact that she accepts me as a friend is incidental to her but is my only link into that situation. Without that friendship I would have great difficulty in maintaining hopes, and I would be pitched into a loneliness that I am afraid of.

R is also lonely and is also isolated. Perhaps I should let her have the car over the winter to prevent her giving up her job. Perhaps if I could do good things, good things would happen to me.

I sometimes think that I would like an honourable exit. A neat touch of bowel cancer or something. I needn't worry then about shaming my kids.

***

Air in the Square

I'm on the edge of mountain country here. Apparently it's scenic from here to Figeac. Then I am going east for a bit, and that should get me into more mountain country at or after Rodez. Not quite the Alps but good riding, and I'm tempted by the Pyrenees. Trouble is, I've got to pick up my bike part from Marseilles airport. That should be a laugh a minute, trying to find the freight department. Marseilles could be interesting. I think I might go for a meal out there. See if we can meet a few people.

41

I've read more David Lodge. I think he keeps the interest up by telling of his sexual adventures – particularly the failures. I'm not sure that you'd be interested in my sexual adventures. I need to have one first. I'm too slow. I sat in the Gambetta in Poitiers one morning and this dripping-in-bracelets female sat next to me, looking, in retrospect, like my kind of sexual adventure. Instead, I rang Sophie in Leatherhead to see how she had got on arranging for my bike part to be shipped to France.

David Lodge doesn't have this type of distraction. Now that his wife has left him in his story, he is discussing his last 'fuck'. Well, he said he could not remember. Well, I can with R. Things were pretty emotional at the time. I wonder what she thinks. I'm going to set off again now, though I am wondering if this theme, if I continued it, would get me somewhere. Perhaps I'm afraid of it.

I'm in Brassac now, on the way to Carcassonne – no trousers on, having coffee and croissant at 4.00 p.m.

My *grand café* came in a jug this time. It's my first food today. Perhaps that's why I've got a headache. The other reasons could be the tail end of this congestion, which is a kind of sinus with ugh, or my being sated by being at my limit with cornering. It seems there's a tendency to try all the time to be at the bike's limit, which, of course, is beyond yours, except that gravel and uneven road surfaces can reverse that.

It being hot, I have a wet, sticky bum, so I'm giving it some air in the square in Brassac. I do have shorts on. I'm not sure whether having my shorts on under leather is better or not. I feel that the more absorbency you have around, the better.

I feel surrounded by Brits here, but I can't be sure.

Since Rodez every town has been more or less deserted but there's still too much noise to hear people talk. There's a guy, who I can't see, in a huge hole in the road, hammering, and there's always a vehicle going by. It's too bloody noisy.

***

Good Feelings

There's been a change in the way I feel. I need to capture it – it's quite a good feeling.

It's a state of equilibrium, where the emotion is not out of control and is more in balance. I'm not sure what is balancing it. Perhaps I'm being too mechanical, and can only see 'balance' in terms of a pair of scales.

Perhaps it's more a pressure system where there is insufficient pressure to lift the valve – less input, therefore less pressure. No, I prefer the scales analogy.

I think what has changed is a human input that was able to restore that balance by putting understanding and kindness on one side of the scale. On the other side, what was there? Fear, trepidation coupled with affection exaggerated? Knowing it was too much it could be met by rejection, or absence.

Past experience or knowledge doesn't help. Rational analysis has no effect on the degree of emotion. Emotion doesn't seem to have any bounds. Why am I not contemplating the 'honourable' exit now? I know that my future is just as uncertain as before, and just as likely to contain loneliness and decrepitude as before.

It must be a realisation that the object of your desire is not to be had and, like a spoilt child, the mind adjusts and seeks other satisfactions.

Women, of course, are difficult to replace or find substitutes for.

I've decided to send 'her' the book. Mistake? Maybe. But what if I die tomorrow and I haven't done it? What if she dies tomorrow and I haven't done it? No, let's make the mistake.

I'm going to talk to Sally first. She knows me. We've been there before – both of us. I don't want anything, well, anything more. I need the attention and companionship and the sharing of a mutual interest: Partheon, a bit of literature, relationships – or lack of them.

All of a sudden, I've this 'pop song' disease – heartache.

I saw Gillian in her shop in Maidstone today and she gave me the list of topics that she has suggested for her conversation evenings. There are twenty-seven. And number twenty-five? 'What is love?' How do you know when it is real? It is claimed that one can love too much. Is this true? Why does it make us feel so vulnerable in this state sometimes, and other times so elated? Why is Gillian asking these questions?

There might be the genetic answer of the enablement of the species to procreate. If it's unrequited, could there be a programming error? Disparate ages should preclude mutual attraction, though the female could select due to the male being successful and likely to give successful offspring. In this specific situation the physical aspect has not been fed, so it doesn't exist and doesn't seem to be a factor. So perhaps the 'heartache' state is an attempt by the instinct to promote physical contact, and thereby create love.

Suggesting that I'm in the grip of some uncontrollable instinctive impulse does not please me. I would prefer that it went away. But it might be too late now, now that the resistance has been triggered. 'She' may be afraid to become involved in future. I'll just have to cope with all the outcomes. I can't influence them – except by being careful not to feed it again.

I do contemplate suicide again. Beachy Head this time. It's not likely because I'm not in a dilemma. I only mention it because the last time began as a casual contemplation of possibilities.

I think I'm reasonably stable and sound, so I'm puzzled that I'm thinking this way. I think that there is a sense of futility in carrying on in an increasing state of lovelessness – love of the kind that females bring, not offspring.

I would like to tell Charlie that I love him. There is a greater need to tell Charlie than to tell my daughter Trixie, though I think that Trixie is just as vulnerable, if not more so.

I would be selfish to withdraw like that, if there are people around who do have a real affection for me. So, it's a bit of a battle between selfishness and giving up hope.

Women are certainly big motivators and spurs to action – another mechanism whose purpose is to protect mother and offspring, perhaps.

***

Villemoustousou

R is always cynical about my 'affair', and it stops conversation. So we can't have these 'quality' conversations that Rosie calls them. Deep conversations require a kind of trust – I can't think of the word right now. I'll work on it. How about 'acceptance'?

It's Tuesday. I'm cold. I still have the 'lurgi'. But the campsite is good, even though I sleep on a slope. It has a swimming pool, and the toilet facilities are mixed sex. I shall investigate Pennautier this morning and perhaps try and see M. De Lorgeril. At present I don't aim to rush off – need recovery time.

My David Gower hat has had its effect here. I think they are suggesting it's African. When I said it was cold they didn't believe it, especially as I'm English. I bought the owner of the campsite a drink last night. I didn't realise they had a shop cum café so I had a beer. He called his wife "*le patron*", so I assume she runs it and him.

There are a few young people on the campsite but mostly they are old – retired. Now that has raised an interesting feeling. I don't know how old they are but I feel that I am young and they are old. I'm not so sure that I'm the same age or not. I looked in the mirror yesterday morning in a more critical vein – that is, not shaving – and I was disappointed. I've got wrinkles under the eyes like bat's wings – kind of curved. They're OK when I smile, but since I don't smile a lot I've got the haggard look.

I wonder whether I'll ever get the chance to say to Partheon what I think – that they told Beryl that I didn't work for them any more, that Urline did not send me the figures, that Clive has made a humiliating offer, and they are generally treating me like a casual employee. I have been much more than that. I can't believe Urline can't see what she's done.

This is coffee time in Carcassonne. Give me Poitiers any time. This place has about as much attraction as Southend. It's kind of dirty and provincial. There are no pretty girls. There are no well-dressed people. The blokes are better looking and more interesting than the girls. There are a lot of strange get-ups. Strange in the sense that you see it all the time in the UK – tights over paunches under T shirts. How can people shaped like that dress like that?

**

Would you believe it, dear reader, she's just rung!

It has not made a lot of difference as far as I can tell. I should be in a state of bliss, shouldn't I?

Well, I'm not. I'm convinced it's a hormone misbalance. I've been to the gym to try and pump out the emotion, but that hasn't worked. What has worked, though, is the intellectual effort of coming to terms with the situation. This is the key. I still feel bad. I have persuaded myself that not writing and not whingeing will prevent an escalation of the emotion, because it is not being fed. So whilst I feel a bit 'edgy', I am developing something of an attitude and slightly different focus.

First, meet more people in a non-business environment and, second, try to meet more women of my own age. This can give me the possibility of warmth in addition to companionship, but she cannot be my lover.

I have to pause at this point, for two reasons. First, given that my last condition is true, can it be expressed? Does it disappoint, whatever the reality? Second, 'can't' and 'never' are negative perceptions but whilst, in reality, they are true, it is possible.

Of course there are physical constraints, and there are considerations of age and circumstances. This is why my intellect suggests a better course for me.

But she is still my friend.

And my Christmas won't be painful any more, though it will be lonely. I can handle it that much better.

I am very fond of her.

Mission Completed

I met M. De Lorgeril this morning. He lives in a chateau. He does 'wine' in a fairly big way, it seems. He's got this lawn of about five hectares and he cuts it with a ride-on. He says this is madness, but there is no well-priced medium-sized kit in France. What the 'fuck' have Partheon being playing at. It was crass stupidity not to deal with French enquiries, especially as I was a free asset for them. I know they had a problem with complementary aspect but you don't solve it by ignoring it and then demoralize it. Spain could be just as attractive too. By attractive, I mean on a *prima facie* interest basis.

I'm in Carcassonne – the new not the old! There's a *toilette* twenty yards from me. It's twenty feet high, with a 'Turkish' type dome. It's only four feet across, and it's cast iron. It must be like an oven in there. Perhaps it costs money and so nobody uses it. On the other hand, it's so hot today there might be no need for it. I've parked my bike in its shadow. Not many bikes in town – not a good sign.

I've just read a bit of Zen. Pirsig has introduced the difference, or dichotomy, between classical understanding and romantic understanding. When I first read this, some years ago, I didn't understand it in the same way as I do now. Strategy in business terms can be classical, or it can be processual or incremental. These processes are in accord with Pirsig. More than that, he describes the type of person involved with each, and those tend to be part of both the classical and romantic - more organic, innovatory.

Pirsig considers, and I can confirm this, that within the classic mode there are romantics who can, seemingly, be frivolous, irrational, erratic. Whilst this is a little extreme, there are benefits. Some of these characteristics are mine, but possibly more are Clive's. So whether it's the differences or similarities within us that give us the affection for one another, I don't know. I could love the guy in a fatherly sort of way. That's what bugs me so much, I expect. We both have enquiring minds, and that might be the key. But Pirsig doesn't mention it. What Clive tells you is different to what he tells others. He can't be trusted, only because he wants to be loved by a particular person and so will change his allegiances. Have I lost out to Roland? From Pirsig's point of view Clive is probably a romantic, but to design a topper requires some cold hard analysis. I'm the classicist, but heavily weighted towards the irrational, and so I have a strong romantic streak. Who else would set off for France to seek two people whose only point of reference, as it turned out, was their postcode? I found that out by asking the first person I saw in France – the baker's wife in Guines. My enquiry went from her, to her assistant, and from her to the guy in *La Marie* – the Town Hall – whereupon I discovered that postcodes have references on the Michelin map. I don't think Clive has the same cavalier approach as me.

Now Pirsig goes on to say, I think, that within, or between, these two understandings, there are people who seem to each to be eccentric. Because they don't fit with either mode, they are considered undesirable, then slightly mad, and then insane. Such unusual behaviour tends to produce estrangement in others, which tends to further the unusual behaviour and thus the estrangement, in self-stoking cycles until a climax is reached.

Did this happen to me and Partheon?

Well, I have an advantage. I can think and read and write about these circumstances and can reach some conclusion. But Partheon, I suspect, will assume they have an answer already. This will reinforce their viewpoint and, as Pirsig sees it, "No one is willing to give up the truth as they see it." Thus no visions of the realities can be unified.

From my perspective, and my MBA training, people will filter out viewpoints that run counter to their own beliefs. This is difficult to contend with. Thus, when I return to England to report and negotiate about my French trip, these factors will be important, and influence the outcome. If we handled this right we might learn a lot, but who wants to learn?

***

I didn't know.

Twelve months, eighteen months – whatever. We had coffee, a drink, a meal, and we were just friends.

Oh, God. I didn't know.

Now, I know.

She was my friend. And I didn't know.

What we had was a common bond. Work. Interests. History. We could share experience and learn something.

Arthur Miller – he was there. Betjeman, and his nymphets.

But she was something else. And I didn't know.

I should have taken note. Filed it away. Put it in my memory banks. Stored the memory. What? I didn't know she would become this feeling, this lovely person, a consuming passion.

Well, I'm glad. Can you imagine not having this?

Where's my magic fairy? Where is she, to take me away and make it better? Make me happy.

But what is happy – feeling miserable or feeling normal? Feeling like crying means you've been there. It's a kind of happiness.

It would be nice to share it. But how remote.

But you've got to tell her. Tell her how it is. But if you didn't know, what are you going to tell her? Now I know.

I'll tell her that I know.[4]

***

Beautiful People

I'm outside the 'café', under a tree, writing at the table, at the campsite. Madame Patron is here and my neighbours have just arrived. He is French and I think she is Dutch – and very attractive. So's he. Perhaps beautiful people do attract beautiful people. Does this mean I'm a beautiful person

---

4 In February 1996 I summarised this piece in two hundred words and entered it in a Radio 4 competition for Valentine's Day love letters. They read out some examples and I thought, "I've done better than that." I received the third prize.

too? People are looking at my hat and me sitting here writing. How do I contend with this? Because it's low-grade material, it's rather pretentious. If it was good I could be rather more assured and dominant. At the moment, the relationship is rather uneasy for me. I will stop and be sociable. *Cà tout.*

It's been a funny day today. But first let me tell you about last night. Hugo and Bridgett invited me back to their tent for a party – well, a drink. I had already told them about my journal and how it came to be called *The Jam and Other Relationships.* Hugo was interpreting this for Madame Patron, who is Catalonian and doesn't understand my French. Nor me hers.

Anyway, Bridgett (Birgit) is German. She is amazing to look at. Beautiful direct eyes and a beautiful smile. And extremely nice. So's Hugo. He's perhaps not as ideally proportioned as Bridgett: she is tall and Hugo is not tall. He's a civil engineer and likes to make decisions. She doesn't do anything right now and cannot make up her mind. They met in America and talk to each other in English.

When we were drinking it was dark, so we couldn't see each other. We discussed the differences between English, French and German people, and whether the French were more decisive because they were more autocratic. I think we generally agreed with this, but I also contended that we needed people and to belong. Bridgett agreed. But Hugo felt we had to make our own way in life and take risks.

> You see, one thing is, I can live with doubt and uncertainty and not knowing. I think it's much more interesting to live not knowing than to have answers that might be wrong.
> *Richard Feynman*

Toulouse

This morning I had to ring M. De Lorgeril in Toulouse. I couldn't make up my mind whether to pack up and camp in Toulouse, or stay another night here. OK. Decision one. Stay here but visit Toulouse. This is in the wrong direction for Trieste and I had this feeling that my decision was bad, especially as it was fifty miles to Toulouse. Toulouse was supposed to be a nice city. Well, cutting a long story short, I couldn't find the city centre because I was in it. Then I could neither park the bike nor find a decent café bar that was not looking out at traffic. Anyway, in a temperature of several hundred, and interminable traffic lights and the odd traffic sign,

I did several obscure circuits. I did stop once but this was at a restaurant, so I decided I'd had enough of Toulouse and got out.

Getting out was another fiasco and I had to go back in again to get out. By this time my bum was getting very sore. I don't know why bums get sore, but I concluded it was a combination of bruising and rubbing. Sitting on a hot saddle was a bit off-putting but soothing too. So at fifty miles from home I was not at all happy about my decision, or about Toulouse.

On top of this, Mr. Lorgeril's compatriot was on holiday, so that was a dead loss. This set-up doesn't seem to me to be quite as right as M. Gesret.

On the way back I made another decision. I would have my coffee and croissant in this village. I passed two likely places with people, and stopped at a third with none – I thought. Before deciding on a *grand* or *demitasse café* I asked for a croissant. Off M. le Patron went and brought back two. He then showed me the figures '18' on the calendar, so I presumed the croissants were *dix huit* francs. I frowned a bit at this. This is five litres of English petrol in real money and I concluded I was in a Spanish bar and they were all cowboys – him, his wife, and Brutus in the corner.

The croissants were tough. I vowed never to go to Spain and I didn't like the look of their eyes – cunning – and I didn't know how to handle the *c'est trop cher* bit if I complained of the price. The coffee, in fact, was quite good, and bigger than normal. So I thought the price was going to be astronomic.

What was it? *Quatorze* – only fourteen francs. With a lot of arm waving and nobody understanding a word, I asked about the *dix huit*.

It's just this moment occurred to me that today is the 22nd and so the croissants were made on the 18th – dix-huit – and were old so they gave them to me free or nearly free. So I'm back on Spain again, OK now – all my prejudices were hanging out, that's all.

I got back to Carcassonne and decided to go to *la cite* – the old part. Well, it looks like the Carcassonne version of Leeds Castle and I couldn't stand the thought of walking round that so I decided to go 'home'. That took two circuits of the town to get out as well. Boy, was I pleased to get back after that.

Now I've walked into the village, bought three quids' worth of fruit and tomatoes, and am sitting in the only bar, drinking coffee. I could have been here all morning and ten pounds richer.

Bars in different parts of France seem to be populated by different breeds.

There's a guy who keeps coming to look at me: baseball cap, Mexican moustache – bushy type, sleeveless shirt, leather bracelet with rivets, jeans and sandals. And speaks Spanish. Now, is he the seedy type, or could he be the bloke I ought to get to know?

I didn't tell you about talking to a guy who was the town's alcoholic. This was at Requista, on the way to Carcassonne. Nobody else would talk to him. We seemed to have a meaningful discussion about motorcycles, the Euro '96 football tournament, and how to get from Castres to Carcassonne. Well, that's what I thought we were talking about. I shook his hand when I left, and made another good impression somewhere in the middle of France. Castres is another place I couldn't find my way out of. The outer suburbs of the larger French towns are pretty uninspiring places: traffic lights, dust and factories.

I've been in France about two weeks and I have got nowhere near Italy yet. This morning, before the sore bum and the heat, I thought I would set off for Trieste tomorrow morning. I'm delaying that decision. But since I've got to go to Marseilles I can see this being a kind of incremental thing. To get to Trieste is going to take effort. And my rear sprocket and chain really ought to be attended to. I'm going to buy some bread now, and go back and read.

***

Perhaps we should analyse the situation in more detail.
I am the medicine man. I've spread my genes as best I could.
The mix of genes could be quite wide, and thus be quite a good
basis for the future.

Other parents may have found like-genes with which to
combine and thus concentrate favourable characteristics. If
you observe my son and daughter, I don't think R and I have
done too badly relative to the starting point.

So having procreated, what is there left for the older generation?
As a 'medicine man' I would have the role of trying to explain
behaviour that did not fit logical interpretation.

Whilst that could be a valuable function in society, it begs the question of how you arrive at that position.

What about the people who need to leave the gene spreading situation but have not yet arrived at the 'medicine man' status?

There is a large gap between procreation and 'medicine man'. What seems to be the case is for fertile females to seek out successful males. Successful males can be of any age – from youth to 'medicine man'.

It is unlikely that females are all sufficiently attractive to be appealing to successful males. Thus less attractive females will possibly settle for less attractive males, on condition there is sufficient comfort for the males to ensure protection and nurture for unattached females and prospective offspring.

My circumstances can no longer offer success or protection, so I'm close to medicine man status – the 'uncle' or 'father' who has experience. That's not what I want to be – it's too lonely.

***

A Most Beautiful Place

I thought I'd stop at this point. I'm 720 metres up in the mountains, about twenty to thirty miles north of Carcassonne. It's still only 10.30. I'm just about at the tree line at a sort of pinnacle of rock, from where the valleys and gorges all around can be viewed. I've been here twenty minutes, and only one vehicle has passed.

It's cloudy but I think that's because I'm in the mountains. There's a lot of purple heather out just below me. It was very hot again his morning – I was late leaving in my attempt to start early and avoid the heat. At the moment I wish I had my hat on to keep warm.

I'm at Roc Suzadou. But it doesn't matter really. Did I tell you that motorcycling is about travelling and arriving at places like this? The fact that I'm on my way to Marseilles is neither here nor there. David Lodge would try and explain or discover the origination of 'neither here nor there', but I'm on top of a mountain.

I can hear bloody music. It's getting louder. I wonder if it's the lead vehicle of that cycling group I passed on the way up. The first vehicle that turned up was a couple of guys with a video camera, taking shots of the view. The next vehicle to stop is the Cyclists des Chateaux Cathares van with four or five non-cycling cyclists. But no music: that's still coming. It's kind of Austrian Tyrol knees-up music. That's what it is – it's going past, it's the lead vehicle telling the world that there's fifty million cyclists coming on behind.

Why can't I hear the music when it's going downhill? Or has it stopped?

My visitors have gone. I should have waved but didn't.

I had this feeling yesterday in the swimming pool at the campsite. I don't know what I'm doing here. It's very detached from the world as I know it, but I do recognise it.

I'm sitting in quite a strong wind but there's a butterfly seemingly making progress against it. Perhaps it's not windy over there. I'll check. Christ, that was close. I nearly lost the page of writing down the mountain. I'll try again for the butterfly.

Well, they do fly against the wind. Not far: they get swept away and then they can get back again. They manage to stay around the same spot.

When you start looking more closely rather than at distances, you see an unbelievable number of different flowers. Not noticeable at first. I think that's because they are not en masse but just in clumps, and kind of fit with the general scenery. There are red poppies, purple flowers, blue flowers, yellow flowers, mauve flowers – well, more than that, really – subtle shades of the same colour.

I seem to be reluctant to leave here. There's no one else around, you see. It would be nice if a few of my friends could share it. Not all at once. Charlie would like it.

I'd like Urline to see it, just to indicate that I do have experiences outside of personal ones, if that describes it. I get the feeling that Trixie might be looking more at me than at the scene. I think R's kind of here anyway. I suppose I'll leave and go. Can't just stop here, and I suppose progress has to be made. Got lots of thoughts crowding in, but I don't know what they are.

Here's another car. Time I went.

***

December 1995

Happy Christmas

If this was literature it would be written as a history or as a fiction, sometime in the future – a possibility. But it's not. It's real time. So there's no merit in that, is there?

They're letters. To someone who might accept them as me.

I've bought Annie Lennox's Medusa *for me this Christmas. I love it. I also bought Barbara Dixon's* Dark End of the Street. *She sings too slowly says Urline, but perhaps fits the essence of the songs.*

Urline's ringing tomorrow, she said! Dare I say it: I love that woman? Do I? Perhaps. If not, why do I feel this way? Is tomorrow my last day of hope? God, please let her not say she can't handle my obsession. What will I say to put her off? I want nothing. Nothing more than what previously existed.

The change is the big clammy hand of demand. Somebody else's affection might be oppressive and, despite her being a caring person, she could find it necessary to free herself of another's affection.
I told Trixie and she was good. Said all the right things – gave me hope. I've yet to tell Sally. Sally's been there and I was close to her at the time. But I didn't realise the hurt she was feeling. So the cuddles were for real. I could have handled it better. I remember those cuddles, Sal.

Anyway, what about tomorrow? It's the end – isn't it? – of all the dreams: having dinner together with my kids, of worrying about Partheon, of talking about Bloke, of being her friend. How can I stop these reflections of the past?

***

Chateauneuf du Pape

I'm really pissed off. Even after the Roc. After the Roc, I passed through some of the best country I've ever been in. I crossed a river and stopped on the bridge to watch people swimming. I thought, let's stop here; this village looks good. But at 12.30, I felt that to travel and see what's next was the thing.

Well, I did this the last time I was in France, in lavender growing country, and regretted it ever since.

From the river the road was good and bendy, and we went well. Even stopped for coffee somewhere. Then came Montpellier, then Nimes. Just like Romford. Dreadful. Very commercial. I got lost again leaving Montpellier. Anyway, I could see that Marseilles was fading and my objective was changing to Chateauneuf du Pape, where Charlie did some summer work.

It was hot. I had made reasonable progress and I decided the centre of big towns was not on the agenda, so I stopped for coffee at a *Centre d'Activité* in Nimes. This is a massive trading estate with shops and bars – a 'buy your carpets here' sort of place. Well, I had my coffee and went off to Chateauneuf du Pape.

When I got there, I went to the tourist office to ask about campsites. "No," she said, "none," in French, of course.

"How about *Auberge de Jeunesse*," I asked.

"No," she said, "none," laughing in a way that suggested that I was thirty years too late. I didn't believe her, so I asked for the paper shop to buy a map.

Catastrophe! When I went back to the bike to find the number of the Michelin map of the area., my glasses were not there. Sod! Sod! Sod!

So, bought the map, looking with my spare glasses. Good job I remembered to bring my spare glasses. Found a campsite – at Chateauneuf du Pape – and an *Auberge de Jeunesse* nearby. Then, off I sped back to Nimes – a sixty-mile round trip to the shop to look for my glasses. To put on my helmet I had put my glasses on the luggage bags, then forgot to pack them. So my glasses went 'the journey'! A very droopy dude!

The campsite is managed by a Chinese-Frenchman, who was very friendly, by the way, and wanted sixty francs for one night. I told him it was *trop cher*. Anyway, he found on his computer that one person was forty-three francs. That's better, I thought. Might stay two nights then.

But the site! It's sand over a kind of pebble hardcore. Putting pegs in was a right bastard. I was hot and getting hotter, and my palm was getting sore – I hate using the spanner for a hammer – and the shops were going to close in half an hour. I kept saying to myself, "Typical French stupidity," but that is counter to what I have experienced this trip, isn't it?

Anyway, I bought some sausage – in a pre-pack this time – and some *yaohurt* and some *pêche*, really to keep the locals happy. I don't need anything. I've yesterday's bread, a big lot of cheese – new stuff – and some dodgy pâté. Dodgy because it smells a bit of the animal, and it's local *Villemoustousou*. 'Local' is always a recipe for getting 'funny' local delicacies.

I'm in the bar now. The waitress might have smiled in her life, but not in my presence. But having lost my glasses and being camped on a stone quarry, I'm going to have another beer. There's a posher place round the corner. Perhaps I'll exercise my customer rights. Christ, they're taking the chairs away – they obviously don't want me. I should charge them for advice on customer care.

I'm at the next bar. The barman speaks English, and he smiles.

I've discovered more about sore bums today. The locus of pain is at the back of the upper thigh and it is not where you sit; it's where you roll when you corner. It kind of 'kneads the bum'. I don't know if the oil helps – I thought it did up to about 200 miles. But the extra sixty to seventy miles to look for my lost glasses put matters back where they were – sore bum.

My cold – sinusitis – is slightly better. Lots of 'running' but much less semi-hard 'Araldite'. Both difficult to get out and it collects without you knowing it. There's always a layer of 'Araldite' where the right nostril and the outside environment meet.

There's two beautiful people in this bar – a fifty-year-old film star: male, tanned and rich looking; and, talking to him, a thirty-seven-year-old female with terrier, in the prime of life, and also a film star. 'Joe's' arrived too, and he's got the biggest gut in France.

Drinking beer in French bars is never a satisfying experience. It's too lonely. I think I'll go home and eat and get ready for Marseilles tomorrow. You can see what's happened here, can't you? I've gone to Chateauneuf du Pape because Charlie suggested it. My own choice without that would have been Marseilles itself. It could have been worse, but having an objective has intervened. I perhaps should have stopped when the mood says "This looks OK" for the intermediate objective. I didn't want to be here.

January 1996

And a Happy New Year

What now? It's 1996. I danced with my wife (ex) last night. I even made a proposition. When I rang her today she said she'd enjoyed the evening. That's a new situation.

I still want Urline to ring though. I don't know why. Is it just a need in a person to have the one who is loved show some kind of affection? Or might things be better to have them continue just as they were?

I've reached a point where I think I've decided to take a trip to Italy and advertise for a female companion. Such an advert could be sufficiently odd to attract somebody interesting.

I rang Sally, by the way. She replied about a week later. She'd been away for Christmas. I know she's young – thirty-four – but it's nice to have a confidante that you know won't let you down. She's invited me up and I think I will go. Her baby's not due until March.

I wonder why I feel like this? It might be straight depression. The doctor told me three or four years ago that this form of euphoria and then feeling down was a symptom of manic depression. I went to the doctor on Friday on the strength of this, but neither of the two that I know was available so I withdrew. I could be just plain silly and need something objective to occupy my mind. I feel better than I did but I still hope that Urline will not give me up as a friend.

I've been playing Barbara Dixon a lot. I think it's fantastic. One or two of the songs are appropriate for me right now. Annie Lennox is good too, but not in the same league. Trixie has brought me Annie Lennox's Diva, *and also Tori Amos. So, I've got some nice female singers to listen to. I don't listen to the serious programmes in the evening now. I prefer to come to the point of tears with this music.*

I've got to cope with real life tomorrow. See the surgeon about my groin, go to the gym to keep in shape, research into business performance measures, and then take some action to earn some money. At the same time, put the bike right and plan for the big escape. I don't know how to escape – I need a woman. I told ex-wife I needed a hug. That's fairly personal stuff but I didn't get ridiculed. I suppose her and me both.

What is a puzzle to me is that Urline can't hug me. Ex-wife could, though. Urline could hold my hand – that would be nice – but that would be about the limit. I've thought about sex but somehow it wouldn't fit. That's why I don't think it's love. I think it's companionship with some touches to signal a shared understanding. With ex-wife we have to contend with history, the spent passions, the awareness of disparities – why did she just throw the sausage meat in the pan instead of moulding it into patties?

I think my relationship with R is spread geographically too far. We need different things from different people, from the group.

I don't like the thought of Urline having sex with another person. This is jealousy of 'closeness'. I want somebody that close – and as beautiful. That could be shared understanding too, couldn't it?

By the way, Urline did ring. She sounded different – more contented, brusque even. She threatened to stop ringing me to enable me to get over my infatuation (my word) but she said it was unfair for her to mention this at the end of her phone call. Anyway, the last thing that she said was, "Speak to you soon."

So, here I am... again.

***

I need to get to Marseille today but I'm stuck in the tent, waiting for the rain to stop. I've already dried the tent out once – hoping. But here we are, 10.15, and, would you believe, the sun is out. It's been thundering all morning. I could go out and come back but this campsite is in a wood and has no appeal at all, so I want out.

I'm not looking forward to the trip to Marseille: it's going to be traffic and heat. Now that I'm going to the airport, the question is, do I go into Marseilles to say I've been? To have this meal I promised myself?

Then I have to decide where to go next. Is it Trieste – to head east to Italy; or a leisurely trip north, with coffee and croissants all the way? I also have a sprocket problem, which I thought I might get fixed somewhere here.

The inside of my tent is yellow, with a blue floor. Yellow is quite good. You get the feeling the sun is shining. There's a blanket on the floor. An absolute must is the blanket – soft, colourful, home from home. Can you imagine having one of those plastic bedrolls? There is an old brown-and-yellow sleeping bag that serves me well. Then, going clockwise, five plastic bags (to keep things waterproof in my tank bag) containing books, oddments, maps, and cutlery tools. Then things in use: my notebook, three maps, a book, a box with food, my leathers as a pillow, my Amnesty International blanket-bag for my clothes. And the empty waterproof bags that hold the sleeping bag, blanket and clothes bag. Close to the entry flap I have trainers, flannels, earplugs, a dirty handkerchief, shorts, pen case, box with my drinking glass, knife, dictionary, and foam pad for cleaning the leathers. I've got to get this lot and the tent packed away now if I'm going to make progress today.

I left Carcassonne, aiming for Marseilles – roughly. I decided to travel to where Charlie spent some time: Chateauneuf du Pape. I know I would have to go, just to say I had been. Losing my glasses was due to needing to read the map and the usual stupid reason of putting them down on my gear and just riding off. Is it really necessary to go through the spectacles, testicles and watch routine before leaving anywhere? I have a horrible feeling it is. Things go wrong.

My plan was to pick up the indicator relay from Marseille airport, and then eat in Marseille.

It was hot. It took time to pack up – we had thunderstorms all around and the tent got wet. So I gave things a lot of time to get dry, wiping the tent down a couple times. I also did my toilet cleaning trick. I wash it for me and then brush it clean for whoever follows. There's no toilet seat on these toilets. Once I'd finished I am washing hands and cleaning teeth, when a girl comes in and walks into 'my' toilet and immediately walks out again and into the next. Why? On inspection I found that her choice was stained but dry; 'mine' was clean but wet. Just thought you might like to know that!!

I found Marseilles airport with no trouble. I found the freight area with even less trouble. Then the trouble started. France Handling said I had the wrong bill number, and Air France said I had the wrong bill number. How can I have? Where's British Airways? Why don't they ring? So I ring 'Assistance' again and find I have – that's right – the wrong bill number. Once I had the right one I got my part without a problem.

Of course, it doesn't work. Well, why should it? How would we know if something worked if sometimes it didn't?

It's Velo Sport, not a Suzuki part, so I'm pretty cheesed off and hot and have to abandon that effort. So I set off for the hills but after about two minutes I say to myself, "I can hear my engine too well. I haven't got my earplugs in. Where are they?" Have I lost them? I was on a slip road to a motorway, so I needed to decide pretty damn quick whether to walk back, or drive on and return to the freight area.

Well, I've not got out of anywhere successfully first time, so I decided to stop immediately and walk back. Fifteen minutes there and fifteen to twenty minutes back. And it was hot.

But I found my earplugs.

Is this a 'success', after the glasses? They were on the concrete where the lorries come in and out, and had been run over. I must have lost them when I ran from the phone box back to the bike to get a pen in order to write the correct bill number. Strange that, isn't it? Somebody in Leatherhead gives you the wrong number and you find your earplugs in the loading area of the freight department of Marseilles airport. Shall we discuss chaos theory sometime? This is nothing to do with butterflies flapping wings in Uruguay, is it? This is not preordained? Is it a straight chance event? There must be more to it than that.

So, with earplugs carefully licked and cleaned, I set off again for a hill – I couldn't face Marseilles in the heat, especially four o'clock when the day is done.

***

I thought that this chapter ought to, or could also be, a letter. This causes all sorts of problems.

None of the preceding chapters has been written with the intention of having a definite and particular reader. OK, there may have been a notional reader at whom I was directing my thoughts, but a real reader? No, that's altogether different.

I would have to be more guarded. Not let this person know that I'm a wimp really, somebody to be avoided, too much trouble, self-centred, nothing to offer in return. But a letter! There's the essential prerequisite of being independent and capable, able to deal with life, no weaknesses, and sufficiently strong and knowledgeable to offer support to others.

Well, that's not the case, is it? It's more the Tate and Lyle story – out of the weak comes forth strength. Well, not quite. Individuals handle weaknesses by dealing with the causes and putting matters right, or at least making things better.

Pairs of people bring a different solution. First, they have disparate experience; and second, they cause each other to consider alternatives which, superficially at least, have to be considered by virtue of their closeness to events. It leads to depression because to have one means to give up the other – to give up the possibility of passionate feelings on the one hand for the possibility of understanding and unconditional acceptance on the other.

OK, so these five paragraphs are a drag; but it's important that I make reference to the fact that letters differ from 'general writing'.

I'm writing to you. We have a history together, a context, plus a further history probably making us act the way we do.

I am very fond of you. I think I love my ex-wife more now than before the divorce. These emotions conflict, but are irreconcilable.

***

Cherries at Bonnieux

I was going to tell you about the day – a pretty bad day on average. *A woman has just walked over and given me a tray of cherries*!! What can you think when this happens but that life has its ups and downs. There must be a better expression than that. I'm in Bonnieux, I think. I'm showered and tidy but have just been in the heaviest rain I have ever seen, plus hailstones. I must finish eating before it gets dark, and at least start on the cherries.

One of the problems with eating the way I do is that I am having a conversation with this journal and all the gems are getting lost. So I've started to write. The 'book' is on the petrol tank. My meal is in a box on the luggage rack. I'm standing by, dressed in winter gear because I'm bloody cold. My 'David Gower' is good for cold too, but I think I've made that point before. If you have a problem reading this it could be that my aromatherapy oil, which I use for my complexion, is on my hands too. I suspect a little gets spread on this paper, and so the pen or ink can't cope, and I have to go over the letter or stroke again.

Have you noticed how wind, apart from being cold, is a pain in the arse? It blows everything about – *you* have just been blown on the ground – and its persistence is plain bloody irritating.

However, given the experience of the last thirty-six hours, we will get through somehow, and it's this I want to tell you about.

February 1996

Doctor, Doctor

Well, I've been to the doctor's. I've kidded her that I'm ill, or, perhaps I've kidded me that I'm ill. I feel better now that I'm ill. I don't want to get better. I want to be ill for a bit. Perhaps I am ill. How do you know? How do you find out?

She's given me some SSR1 – a chemical that the brain needs in order not to be confused.

I mentioned this, didn't I? I thought it was a hormone misbalance brought about by exclusion from the group. Well, if they don't know for sure, then my theory is as valid as theirs.

Perhaps we do need a target, an objective, an aim. No, I don't want an aim – I want to be. Now.

I'm going to Cyprus next week. That's an objective. And I'm taking me. When I get there it'll be me that arrives. Complete. Problems, solutions, rigidities and quests – the original matrix – two-dimensional. If it was three-dimensional we would make it dynamic – experience, imagery, conceptualisation, confusion.

I wonder if it's coffee poisoning.

I've got a horrible feeling that Urline has bought a 'wrong' car. I don't want that; I don't want her hurt any more. That's an unusual feeling, isn't it? Most often we only want or have these feelings for ourselves. The altruistic mode is not normal.

Still, my Sprint was wrong, but I got a lot of pleasure from it, and it only went wrong at the end.

***

Par le Pont d'Avignon

I abandoned the writing at Bonnieux. It was too bloody cold and windy.

Now I'm at the snack bar, drinking coffee at the Avignon campsite just across the river – the Rhone – from *LE PONT*! Le Pont St Benezet Chatelet.

France are playing Holland.

I have drunk half my Chateauneuf du Pape at below room temperature. Let's try and recap.

France have just beaten Holland on penalties.

From the airport I headed due north and passed two towns and villages with campsites. For some reason, I didn't fancy them. Or was it that Bonnieux was more appealing because of its name? I could see dark clouds around me. I could even hear thunder. I thought, it couldn't happen to me; I'll push on. Bonnieux is on top of a mountain. About a mile from Bonnieux I had to stop because it started to rain; I stood under a tree but it was no good – it was just as wet. So I put on the oversuit, or tried to. Bloody zip gets stuck and I did some cussing. But soon I decided that I may as well ride in the wet as stand under the tree in the wet. There are hailstones the size of marbles, and there is heavy rain – I mean heavy. I set off into a river. I couldn't see. I was doing about 10 m.p.h. to make the upper end of the village, with water pouring down the street in torrents. I went past a café bar but then I decided to stop. I attempted to turn round but the twenty yards through a deep bit was too much for the bike. It stopped, fortunately not in the river. I have to walk back on my heels to try and keep my feet out of the water to get to the bar.

There I am, wet, no bike and no idea where the campsite is, and in the biggest storm this century. It's also unpleasant in the bar because everyone is inside. Most are standing up to shelter from the rain, and the bar is full of tobacco smoke. The bar staff are concerned about something, and it seems that a lot of water has come into the bar and it's behind their large refrigerator. During this kerfuffle the electricity keeps going off. When it sorts itself out I do some worrying over a cup of coffee. What do I do without the bike?

Then what? I go back to the bike and, would you believe, it starts! It could have been petrol – the gauge indicated that it might be. On the other hand, it may have had sufficient heat to dry out wet parts. So I set off again to the village and so to the campsite. There I buy bread, cheese and beer, and pitch on a relatively dry site. It is OK.

It took a long time to unpack because I needed to check for wet gear, and hang it out or separate it from the dry. Was it this that prompted my neighbours to give me cherries?

From a position of "What the fuck do I do now?" to a situation not far from perfect, all in the space of about an hour – I consider to be "pretty fucking damn good."

***

I feel better. I wonder if the drug is having its effect. They said a fortnight but it's only been a week. It 'improves' the brain chemistry and enables the user to see the situation more clearly and make decisions regarding future actions.

There's another explanation, which could be 'as well as' rather than 'instead of'. I said to Urline that I wanted her to ring me, and so didn't mind her ringing me on minor accounting matters.

This gave me the opportunity to express my affection, and the effect was quite dramatic. Suddenly, instead of an inertia and a depressed attitude, I was able to switch to doing some work with some enthusiasm.

I've had another experience. This evening I went to the Singles Club and Daun (Dawn) came up to me and told me a little about herself. She is twenty-eight, and an occupational therapist dealing with mentally handicapped children. She told me she was unhappy, a mess. Later, she told me she was a manic depressive and taking several drugs, and was on a course of injections as well. I tried my counselling skills and found I needed practice. I got a kiss goodbye. Odd. Perhaps that experience has had a beneficial effect too.

Perhaps I should tell you this in more detail. I can't remember properly and so it would probably be boring. It's enough to say that this was like two lost souls meeting in the night and going on their way. No doubt I'll see her again.

I would like to see her again. But I don't want to build a strong relationship.

There was another woman there who seemed quite attractive. But she was sitting in a group – it's a disadvantage to be seated in a group as politeness tends to restrict moving around.

***

Nipples

I didn't finish telling you about the cherries, did I? My chauvinist remarks will horrify most women but I noticed the couple almost opposite me in the Bonnieux site. He had long muscular legs and short shorts. Her legs were similar – from the knee down anyway – and she said hello as they walked by. Probably Dutch. They went for a walk later and when they returned I noticed her nipples were standing out a lot. Unusually so, I thought. I'm not an expert on nipples. I remember one of the speakers, a long time ago, at Speaker's Corner, Hyde Park. He was standing on a newspaper, looked straight at me, eyes wide open, and said, in a very authoritarian manner, "No nipples!"

But, back to cherries. Her shirt was forming round her breasts because of the wind. They looked like pretty good breasts to me. They were a mature couple – I'm not talking dolly bird here. This has taken a long time to write, but it was only an instant in time, an impression. Then, during my meal, she came over and offered me a basket of cherries. I didn't notice her breasts or nipples at that moment. I was struggling with the French for "Thank you. Do you mean just one or the whole lot?" I took the lot. They had been washed. I didn't know whether to eat them all or not. For a while I waited for the couple to return – they'd gone out again – then I ate the lot. There were about two pounds. Then I worried about my movements the next day, both bowel and biking.

In the morning it rains but there's this strong wind that dries everything except my gloves. The tent is difficult to pack up because of the wind, but I manage. Well, you do, don't you?

March 1996

Vacillation

I haven't written for a while. No emotional hype. Nothing to report?

Well, there is. I found my lost photographs of L & K after a serious search. Looking back like this didn't raise any regrets, or nostalgic feelings for what was or what might have been. This was a happy interlude in my life, with a long consequence.

I'm going to show my photographs, plus the little messages, to Urline sometime.

I'm looking forward to going away. To Cyprus. One week. Could get the chance of some funny business but the pills I take don't augur too well for a satisfying performance. But I might get some enjoyment in looking and trying.

Seems I'm building some momentum for the big journey – the great escape. I've been reading some Thoreau. He seems to be advocating the journey into the unknown, the future, rather than to reside in the past or the present. Doesn't have an aim – just uses his instinct as to what direction to take. He seems to be critical of villagers, who, by definition, have not travelled. Conversely, those who travel, constantly heading into the west, are developing their intellect and building their creativity by their contact with nature.

I think I'll ring Sally.

She's not in.

This was a kind of 'thank you' call – I can't imagine her not being around and friendly.

I'm puzzled by the nature of my friendships. Sally is thirty-four; Alec, whom I'm going to see in Cyprus, is about twenty-four. I do have some friends who are older than me – Alan is about fifty, John is about fifty, Woody is my age, but they don't seem to be quite as close. I cringe a bit when I think of Sally and Alec having this older friend. What's in it for them? I don't feel old so I don't feel uncomfortable, but when I stop to reflect on it, it seems odd.

I haven't told you about Urline, have I? Well, she's there.

Not given up hope yet. She's taken my tapes – Arthur Miller and Barbara Dixon – but gave me a pack of coffee. And she wants a print of a picture painted by Susan Seddon Boulet.

So, I'm nearly content. Just anxious. But that could be the side effect of the pills. I don't think so though. I'm in bed now – very early. I couldn't stay up because of this 'anxiety'.

I'm still not sure about this 'illness' – the depression. Am I allowing it to happen, and giving myself permission to give up?

I saw some television briefly tonight and heard this woman, a doctor, who had given up research to go into a job helping handicapped and disadvantaged kids. She claimed that she had been helped in this decision by God. That's interesting, isn't it? Following her instinct and relying on God to take care of her.

I'm not thinking like that. Wouldn't it be irresponsible if I went away on what could be a whim, a loosely held wish to do something pleasurable, and hope that God would help out when I found myself in difficulty? Perhaps the difference is the purpose of the journey and the decision.

The purpose isn't just pleasure; it's 'let's go west and see what life has to offer'. I might find myself doing something equally fulfilling. There is the view that all of us have an obligation to be happy – it makes for a happier situation for all.

***

Gonzalo Plays Flute

The bloody bells are pealing and Gonzalo Vera is trying to play the flute. I'm in the square facing the Palais du Pape, drinking coffee and eating croissant. It's cost £3 but I do have Gonzalo. I gave Gonzalo a franc. Do you think that if I'd given him five francs the coffee would have been better? Christ, here's an *Aphyxes de Blesses* coming by with loud horn. Looks like an ambulance.

Has the man no taste? He's drowning the flute, or is it the horn, concerto.

Just had the waiter wanting money, so I told him his coffee was rubbish. Didn't do any good though. Still, I'm glad I've created this relationship. They're cowboys with a good location.

And!! And. I've had thieves in the night. One nicely washed shirt, a pair of socks, five bottles of beer and, I thought, my half bottle of Chateauneuf du Pape. But I found that in the site next to me. I also found one sock this morning in the road next to mine – it's a big campsite.

That morning was when the wind started – the Mistral – but I got the tent packed better than expected. It dried most gear except my gloves, and made life otherwise a bit awkward.

 I rang Assistance. Hey! There's a bloody train running through the square. This place is geared up for Americans and Germans. I'll find a better cup of coffee in a minute. Assistance arranged for me to go to Avignon Nord to have my bike looked at.

There's something missing in my sense of finding things. I needed to find the *Zone d'Activité*, Centre Commercial, Avignon Nord. Avignon Nord is not signposted – this address came from Paris, by the way – but I found three Centres Commercials, all in Avignon Sud, so I discovered. I asked, and still got lost, but found the directions to the *Information de Touriste*. They were closed until two, so I had a coffee and croissant, which was good but Fr19.50. I set off to try another café. There, a guy in the toilets asked me if I had a Harley Davidson! Is this a coded question?

The tourist information gave me directions to north Avignon. There I ended up in the biggest shopping centre I've ever been in. No bikes though, so I went into a trinket shop to ask. I expected that it could be the kind of shop where English might be spoken. The shop owner rang up the place I was supposed to be and gave me directions. I still couldn't find it. Why? It was a *deponnage*, not a bike shop. A *deponnage* is a road assistance company. No showroom, no bikes. Anyway, they tightened the chain to no effect, and then gave me 'good' directions to the Honda agent in Avignon. They couldn't find a Suzuki dealer! "*Cèst simple*," she said. Whilst I was there she was laughing and smiling, so I asked if she smiled all the time. She said she always did. We shook hands and I left. Aren't I just a slow pillock?

Could I find this place? Could I hell. I even asked a police biker, just around the corner. He waved. Follow *autres directions*. No success. I ended up in town, came across a Suzuki car showroom, and I stopped. The assistant was selling a car. So I waited. Then, I think, the owner turned up. It seemed he came in because a Suzuki motorcycle was parked outside. Although I said I was looking for Honda, he wheeled this Yamaha Virago out of the showroom and lead me round the corner to the Suzuki dealer.

Can you beat that?

The dealer told me it was the chain 'fatigue'. I would not be in any danger but to fix it would be Wednesday. Today is Sunday, by the way.

I found the campsite first time and decided it was the night for a meal in town. But in the camp supermarket I found Chateauneuf du Pape at sixty-seven francs. Other wines were forty, thirty, twenty-five, and the camp plonk twenty-three francs. There was Herault at Fr8.50. So I bought the Chateauneuf du Pape, which will complete my obligation to Charlie, and decided to eat in. If I hadn't, would I have washed the shirt and hung it on the line?

So, here we are, Avignon, opposite Palais du Papes at the 'Café IN and OFF'. but my French is bad – Rip-off, I prefer – where Gonzalo is still knocking it out. Pop classics, but nice.

***

Dear God. Urline. I wish you could read Thoreau along with me. We could share it, then talk about it. I don't know whether that would do us any good but I need another viewpoint on the "society of useful ignorance", which Thoreau calls "beautiful knowledge".

I don't know if such a thing interests you. But we could find out.

I'm not well. I've collapsed mentally. I've no desire to do anything – well, not quite. I know I should do something but I've got a positive disregard for action. This letter is a compulsion. It's almost like walking – a displacement activity.

Thoreau has triggered the need. He proposes that man should not be fully cultivated. There should be an uncultivated part, a mucky bit, which makes the soil deeper. I like that. Perhaps a bit of swashbuckling is allowed. Well, before it's too late, let it happen!

I don't know if you want to talk to me. I don't know that you don't. It seems a pity I shouldn't talk to you. I like to. There's a piquancy about it. It's not quite close. Talking is not enough. It's better than not, and it has retention. It stays in the memory.

***

It's 5.15. I've decided to eat out tonight. Let's do it early rather than at the last minute with no choice. So I've found a nice little place with nice tablecloths and a reasonable price. So, at 7.00 for 7.30, I'll be there. I've come back to the campsite and had a beer and two shots of Chateau. I've polished the bike a little, put on my tight jeans and my grey T shirt, and I'm going poncing about Avignon on my bike. It's windy, cool and very sunny. OK, sunny. I'm not surprised the Pope moved from Avignon – he'd never keep his hat on. This bloody wind doesn't stop. It perhaps explains why the Palais and the castles are so strong, and why the bridge here – *Sur le pont, d'Avignon* – is only halfway across the river. I bet it's really windy in the middle of the river, so they stopped. The bridge doesn't go anywhere, except to this campsite – and that's a den of thieves – so I suppose they thought enough was enough. Silly, isn't it? Humour doesn't fit. Better to talk women.

I had a better cup of coffee in the afternoon, served by a Spanish-looking lady with lipstick – pinkish, and outlined in brown. She smiled at me. Why is that important? Well, at Chateauneuf du Pape the girl didn't. Am I gauging receptions by smiles?

I've just come back from the Palais du Pape and, just a square up from where I thought there was gunfire this morning, is where the youth of the town display skateboard skills. Quite extraordinary; they seem to defy gravity and the laws of science by getting these things in the air. There must be a physical law, like there is in cycling, which God specifically designed for the activity. In motorcycling there is a law of precession. This, I think, is that a tilted, rotating disk heads towards the centre of a circle. Also, if you turn to the right, the disk will lean to the left. So you go towards the centre of the circle. So you turn left, all leant over and by moving the handlebars to the right. Well, that's specific to motorcycles, isn't it? But skateboards need something else. I'm going to get ready for dinner.

Restaurant 'La Ferigoulo'. Not part of the tourist scene. Was that a good decision? Nice meal – ninety francs – plus wine and beer and coffee, a hundred francs. Odd relationship. Still got half a bottle of wine left though. I suppose it was a dear way of buying half a bottle of wine, but I didn't want to run short of alcohol despite being on the bike. Hot cheese on toast – 'St Moncellin' – with salad, then veal and vegetables and then chocolate cake with English cream. I asked what 'English' cream was but the waiter didn't know, other than it was 'English'. I think it was double cream with sugar. Everything was nice except the weak coffee.

The reason for me choosing this particular restaurant, apart from it being 'not tourist' but inside the city, was because the tablecloths were beautiful – and the napkins.

***

Dear Baroux,

This is very hurried and I hope it will be legible. I am sad our friendship has changed, has had to change. I miss it too!

But I had to withdraw because I didn't want to be responsible for your pain. If I have appeared cold and hard it is because of fear – fear of a situation that I could no longer handle. But if your feelings are/were as written in 'Mrs Robinson', I feel humble, unworthy and honoured. I do not want to diminish or demean your feelings by being cold and harsh but I know I can never reciprocate, which is sad. I enjoyed/enjoy our discussions on books and life. I wish you were still my friend. You were very kind. Perhaps in the future we can be mates once more. In this life friendship is important. Yours was important to me. Baroux, you are so clever – talented and aware. One day I should like to read your book – all of it. This is not a permanent state of distance. You're are a good man. You need to find peace.

Go and see Sense and Sensibility. *It's fun. Go to an evening*

class on 'Literature'. Go to the theatre – see The Glass Menagerie *by Tennessee Williams. Tap the rich resources of literature. I WILL DO MY DEGREE. It will never be a good pass but I'd like to do it anyway. I wish I were as clever and astute as you are. I'VE NEVER WON A COMPETITION. I'll see you soon.*
Urline

P.S. I think I am slowly finding peace. Bloke is kind, gentle, accepting and real. It is good to find a soul mate in this life!! I'm very lucky.

***

It's too much. Life is too difficult. I have a letter. A contribution to the book – an even-numbered chapter. A confirmation that Urline cannot reciprocate. But I don't mind that – I know that. It's better that way.

I win both ways. There's no responsibility when she can't reciprocate, but I still have the feeling. I don't know what it is – well, I might, but I don't feel quite grown up saying it. Yearning – meaning two: the feeling of affection or tenderness. That definition is not too bad actually; it comes close to being an apt description without falling back to 'love'.

Love is wrong, even though it's difficult to define. What I think is happening is what is very nice – a maturing of the relationship. With a bit of luck we can learn to cope, with a fondness which is requited.

The difficulty is that there is an imbalance of affection and she, in this case, finds it too much or intense. But if there is an understanding of what each is feeling, and we can feel the limits of that feeling, then perhaps some kind of harmony and enjoyment of the relationship can be achieved.

I haven't told you that page sixteen was précised and became a love letter to 'Mrs Robinson' for the competition in the Afternoon Shift. *I thought it was going to win, but it came third. I'm still delighted. I'm doing battle with the BBC now in order to obtain the letters that came first and second.*

The Big Issue *had a good poem this week. I keep reading it to try and understand what it means. I'm sure it means that the relationship has been achieved but it's right on the edge of it being lost.*

Almost
by Jeanette Ju-Pierre

> *Almost as if*
> *it is too late for words,*
> *for excuses made at the end of*
> *an affair,*
> *for regrets about what should*
> *have been,*
> *never was.*
>
> *Almost as if*
> *it is too late for games,*
> *for situations of opportunity,*
> *which passed right under your*
> *nose,*
> *for the taste of forbidden fruit.*
>
> *Almost as if,*
> *it is too late for life,*
> *for making decisions which*
> *would change*
> *a lifetime.*
> *For journeys to countries where*
> *you*
> *experience déjà vu*

Almost as if,
Almost as if,
it is too late to say goodbye
to another life.

***

Vaucluse

Today I got up, got showered – in the morning! – too bloody cold yesterday. This morning is freezing too, so it's full leather gear with pullover. I'm off to Mont Ventoux – 1900 metres. On the way I arrive at a big street market at Bedoin. Can't get any money – stupid bloody system – so I spend my sixty francs on soap smelling of *verveine*! (I did ask but I'm none the wiser except it has a yellow flower), some peaches from a guy who told me he has a VFR, some cheese, some bread, and some pâté. I also had a coffee – the worst yet. I nearly bought some wine but the guy wouldn't take a cheque. "I do not know this way of buying," he said.

So, up to Ventoux, and I see the Alps from a high point, and all the surrounding mountains. I didn't know there were so many mountains in the east. Anyway, impressive and a good ride, but nothing like the feeling of Roc Suzadou, so I leave fairly quickly and go down with a group of bikers – pedalists! – who go down at 25 m.p.h. when it's bumpy and 40 m.p.h. when the going is better.

***

Carpentras

I've arrived at Carpentras and got some cash, and am sitting under shade in the square, looking at a church, with people walking by. Since it's now 2.00 p.m. things are more busy – not a lot more, but more than when I got here half an hour ago. There's a group of people around here who are a bit dusky, with round bridges of the nose. That's Arab, isn't it? There are some beautiful women and girls here. Does an attractive town entice attractive people? There's a GSX R 1100 parked by this café. Silver and pink. People might think that it's mine! Nice to be associated with it. In the UK you couldn't park a bike in the square like this. It could be that the French have a passion for bikes, which like the people, are nearly all beautiful – and female!

I don't feel that I should describe the square to you, but it gives such a good feeling I could try. It's rectangular and fairly small. On the long side is the church. To its right is a big three-story sandy-coloured official 'Napoleonic' building – well, it couldn't be Regency, could it? Opposite it are three cafés, one bank and two or three shops. One shop has these beautiful 'Provence' type dresses on rails. At the ends are shops with flats above with wooden shutters, mostly closed. In the middle are two pools, with water running out of the 'Greek's' mouth. The Suzuki is by a pool with beautiful people walking by – male and female and kids. There's a kid splashing at the pool, a couple having a wrestling kiss on the other side, and a group of lads sitting on the church steps. I can't believe what's going on here. The sun is chasing me round the shade but I can't move because if I did I wouldn't be able to see 'out'. A woman walked by just now – a native – with red hair, short. Her trousers were rust coloured. Her waistcoat was wool, with a deep brown border. The rest was whitey creamy beige. It was knitted, with loops and things. She wore jewellery. Not a great beauty, but everything seemed right and was totally attractive.

I think what it is, is the absence of crowds and the absence of yobbos. There's a group eating salad, and I fancy trying to imitate it. Now that I'm in funds, and it's nearly three o'clock, I'll go back to Avignon and the big supermarket, and find some salad. Alternatively, I could buy lettuce and tomatoes and chop them up. But I need a plate and some dressing, don't I? There's that redhead again. I've got the colours wrong but it doesn't matter. She's smoking. Every woman in France smokes. It's a good job you can sit outside.

I wonder if today is the day for an ice cream? Oh, I nearly forgot – last night I read some Ben Okri. You must read Ben Okri. How do people perceive so well? I'll tell you more if I can, later.

The wines I shall record the names of are: Clos de L'Oratoire des Papes 1992, L. Amouraix, Chateauneuf du Pape, Domainedes Riot, Côtes du Rhône, St Michael-d'Euzot, Domaine de Murmurium, and Côtes du Ventoux.

***

I went to the pub – a kind of continuation of my birthday spend-up – but also to read Lesley Glaister and my other purchases.

I was concerned that I had made a poor purchase. I didn't feel good about Lesley Glaister, just because I had heard her book reviewed on the radio with the title The Private Parts of Women.

I had also looked at Proust and Updike. Well, everybody ought to read them, shouldn't they? Proust was three inches thick, and that was only volumes 1 and 2. No wonder there's merit in that. Updike had knickers and flies and sexual intent. I felt stamina and sex were the wrong reasons for purchase so I declined – I didn't have the urge.

But nor did I with Lesley Glaister, but perhaps it was my persistence to find it. The two assistants took a long time to trace it, even though both had seen it. The Private Parts of Women *is not the best title for a man to be interested in when the book is hard to find.*

However, I also bought some Blake and Kafka and Nietzsche, which salved my conscience a bit.

So I went to the pub for escape. Urline had arisen like a phoenix, and cut my future down to the next two days. If a friend decides she doesn't want you as a friend you must move on and find another. I suppose Susan Jeffers said that. I wasn't going to quote people, but I need to because I need to disagree.

Whilst friends can give you up, their existence within your soul remains. There's no casting out. I must fill up my garbage bin of history with loves, acts, ideas, shame, secrets.

It's no good dying with it half empty. Nothing do I treasure so much.

I was reading Lesley Glaister and came close to tears. She uses this beautiful short sentence. She talks to my soul and touches 'edges' – my raw nerves. I love my book now. I'll send it to Urline. I don't think she'll cry, though.

Her garbage can is alive. Maybe Bloke is looking out. I wonder if she's read Stevenson: "Once we've seen somebody from another perspective it's difficult to ignore it."

That is intellectually satisfying but I can't say that I've experienced it. My opinions have not changed – my friends seem to grow more faceted and with more reasons to love them.

I read Lesley Glaister and composed this letter or its idea at the same time. And cried at the same time. In the pub.

Remember my 'love letter' with the "I didn't know" phrase in it? Well, read this from Glaister:

***

BOY

It is time to come out
I have been asleep but now I am awake
I want to come out now and... I don't know what
I don't know how
I am shouting to Trixie and moving my arm
She will not hear me
I am stuck in Trixie
And she will not know

***

Smoking Women

I've never seen so much food. I'm in Auchon, I think. Avignon Nord. This is a shopping mall in which there is a huge supermarket with food and drink I've never seen before. It's in such huge quantities I don't know how it's all sold. The mall itself is in a *Zone d'Activité*, I think – another big area where trading is done. I don't think it's industrial.

This morning it was very cold again. Took my bike to the bike shop and asked them to stop the noise from the chain and sprocket. It's going to cost just over a thousand francs, of which a hundred and sixty is labour. I think that is cheap. If it is, how does the average mechanic buy his bike and buy petrol? It seems to me, looking at prices, that food and drink can be very good even at the less expensive end. I bought garlic sausage this morning for Fr17.60 per kilo. My 'usual' type *saucisson rosette* is about seventy francs.

The people in the bike shop couldn't be nicer. I could live here. Yesterday, in Carpentras, I bought some Provence cloth. It looks so attractive. I know it was for me – a scarf to wear when I'm biking in hot weather. It's perhaps too good. It cost Fr120 – about £14. Perhaps I should buy presents for others – Trixie and R. I'd like to buy tablecloths. I still might. If I can spend this money on the bike, what's a few more quid for some nice furnishings? When you come across something that you consider is nice, there's a kind of 'ache' feeling – the pleasure of 'knowing', sharing in something good. Like the Suzuki and the square in Carpentras. My scarf isn't quite perfect maybe, or maybe it is. It's royal blue with, God, what's the colour between red and blue? Not mauve – deeper than that – with some red and some yellow and some, well, it's not here, it's at the tent. Provence seems to favour rosebuds – at least that's what I think they are – so the scarf, or cloth, uses this basic design feature and then adds to that. Purple. That's it, between mauve and purple – a kind of browny-purple. It's rich and lovely. Because it's not perfect, perhaps I love it better – more – better. Urline said I was obtuse. Well, I'm confusing myself now. How about a little Ben Okri now that we're into words.

Auchon, le Poitet is where I am, said the waiter. It's good coffee. So I have some more and try to discuss Okri's *Birds of Heaven*. One of these 60p booklets – two inspirational essays. I've only read a few pages – it was overwhelming. If you are reading my stuff, stop now. Read Okri.

He is saying that words are insufficient. There is a beyond. A meaning that comes from art and from being. I don't want to paraphrase. I wouldn't do it justice. This isn't an exam. Nor should I copy it out. But I would like to give a couple of examples:

"...a bump on the head may pass away, but a cutting remark grows with the mind."

and

"We are all wounded inside in some way or other. Which is why we need a little gentleness and healing from another. Healing in words, and healing beyond words. Like getting warm gestures like friendship, which will always be a mystery. Like a smile, which someone described as the shortest distance between two people."

and

"...a young woman, standing on a shore, looks out into an immense azure sea rimmed with a silver line of the horizon. She looks out into the obscure hearts of destiny, and is oddly overwhelmed by a feeling both dark and oddly joyful. She may be thinking something like this: 'My soul looks forward and looks forward and wonders – just how am I going to get across.' That is beyond."

There's yet another beautiful girl come into this *brasserie* and starting to smoke. There's a guy at the next table who, like me, is totally transfixed. He's had another cup of coffee. It's just a sodding shopping mall but I'm in a bloody dream-world here – everybody is beautiful. I would like to ask her – I nearly got up and asked another girl – why so many girls in France smoke. It must be more than 80 per cent.

Well, feel the fear and do it anyway. I've asked her. Her mate turned up so I felt safety in numbers, and put the question. They were a bit confused at the question, but could only shrug their shoulders.

So. One and a half hours in Avignon, and two coffees and a croissant: thirty-three francs – about £4. I've become accustomed to the price. Better I do feel after a decent cup of coffee. I'm now looking forward to my pâté, meat, cheese and wine. I think I'll take the bike to the shop, then spend two or three hours in Avignon buying some bread and walking round generally. I'm troubled by this. Is this just a dull shit? The point about a bike trip is the travelling, making progress, covering ground, taking the corners, seeing what comes next. Looking forward. But I've also got this feeling that instead of travelling I could stay put and try these cheeses and breads and wines. Perhaps, most of all, make some relationships. My plan at the moment is to persist with Trieste.

Half an hour later and I'm in Orange. I'm in another square, but it's triangular this time. I've just bought four serviettes in Provence pattern – twenty francs each. Salve my conscience a little. The lad spoke to me a lot in French, me in English, sort of mixed, and he gave me an apricot. We were talking about soap and the different perfumes. One was apricot. I sat down for a coffee – what else? – in the square, and five young people came and asked for money. They seemed nice people. I gave them two francs. Just paying for the experience (or for the apricot). I ought to try to avoid brackets and just use dashes and commas.

I saw an ice cream just now. What do you think? Shall I have one? How do you say "Can you spare a dime? in French? '*L'argent, l'argent*'?"

***

Dear Urline, I don't love you. But I do. You've rejected me and I need to come to terms with this. You're not my type – I'm not yours, I mean. But that's not important. My edges have been penetrated and made raw. I'll have to put these feelings in the garbage can and pack up and go. That's why you cry in the pub: it's knowing without knowledge.

***

Breakfast at Les Halles

It's not ten o'clock yet. I'm in Les Halles, an indoor market. The natives are drinking beer and wine. I have just spoken to my 'neighbours' – two people, by the way. They have had duck for breakfast, and are going to drink a litre of Côte du Rhone between them. I've just bought a huge croissant but it's more like tea cake. It is tea cake. The coffee was good – ranks with Angers.

I was going to write something profound today. I've got all day in Avignon. My neighbours are drinking champagne now with Madame Patron. By the way, this is the French equivalent of an English 'greasy spoon', but seems to be transported into a high class restaurant by the friendliness. More champagne.

OK, profound. What does it mean? I thought I'd start to write before I thought. That seems to be the right way round. Profound is interpretation from a peculiar perspective. I'm a little put off as well as inspired, by Ben Okri. I think you need something to say that makes a contribution to life. We need to pool our thoughts, sift them, and try to draw out that which has meaning from that which was needed in order to get there. To get "across", as Okri says, and get "beyond".

Although he wants to get beyond meaning, it's the 'ache' I have this morning. Something beyond and is expressed by this market. Good products enjoyed by good people.

I thought my neighbours got up to go. I think they did but they took their glasses to the counter and are drinking more champagne. I wonder if I should join them and have a glass of rosé. I'm supposed to be in a café on a pavement, watching whoever goes by, but here I am, getting stoned in Les Halles market. My neighbours are kissing Madame Patron goodbye, and here in Avignon it's a three-kiss routine. In Poitiers it is four kisses – two people, two cheeks. The mathematics, for me anyway, is that each person kisses an opposite cheek making two kisses, so if you do that again to the other cheek that's another two, making four. So three kisses begs a few questions, but how can I ask that? Which cheek is first? Which gets two? Oh Gord! I've just looked up French kiss. I give up. I've just made eye contact with the girl in the *charcuterie*.

I'm at the end of the writing notebook. Rather than turn it over and start on the reverse side, I'm going to buy another one. I will feel better if I don't write on both sides of the paper. Then we can get back to the profound. By the way, I'm a grandfather to a granddaughter called Josephine. *Au revoir*.

I spoke to a lady in the café-bar of Les Halles. She was about seventy. I asked her if her skirt was typical of Provence – *à la mode de Provence*. She, and her husband, I think, said it was 'strict' Provence. It was blue and white, beautiful, full and pleated. I showed them my scarf but they indicated that it was not typical of Provence – perhaps more *touristique*.

I'm in a restaurant now for coffee. They didn't have croissants. I just fancied this place. I was wrong. It's quiet, with people eating in relative silence. The married kind. Nothing wrong with that. As Okri says, silences convey meaning and 'go beyond'. But I feel the environment warrants more animated discussion.

Les Halles will be closed by now. Perhaps I've lost the chance of another particular bread – cooked slowly over two days.

I've bought two bottles of good wine – one for the bike shop and the other for me to know what it is like.

I bought the wine in Les Halles, at a specialist wine stall. Brandy at £30. Plum brandy. He recommended rum and dark chocolate and moonlight and a friend.

I'd like to eat what these folks are eating – about £8 to £9 excluding wine. I don't think too many meals alone are a good thing. I'll continue to wander round. Perhaps have an ice cream at the Spanish lady's.

I've bought another pad for this journal – 'Rosie's' is full – forty francs, which is about £5. I wonder what Rosie paid for the first one – I didn't think they'd be that expensive – and Rosie's is better than 'mine'.

The bike has cost Fr1785 (£220), plus the bottle of wine.

I took the wrong turning out of Avignon to go to the supermarket, and ended up in a bar in Villeneuve. Now, what do I do with all that beer at home?

I've been checking back at some of my writing and I sometimes have trouble recalling where I was. Does this matter? You certainly won't know. It's not the town so much as whether I'm in a bar, the tent, the campsite, en route, or on my second or third stop.

This is my third session today. I don't think it matters enough for me to go back and fill in some of the gaps. On the other hand, to try and remember the tree under which I was eating in Trémorel might be nice for the future. Nice, but not important? Well, it could be important. I chose the site because of that tree.

Why this bar? Well, in front of me is an old church tower: square, castellated, weathered. But I didn't choose the bar for that reason. I chose it because in a minute the sun will appear from behind the tower, and I'll be sitting in the sunshine.

But at the moment there are also two buses letting off pneumatics and pushing fumes into the environment, and creating a traffic jam.

France are playing Czechoslovakia at the moment. It's 0-0.

Am I going to spend more money and celebrate Josephine by going over to the *boulangerie* and buying a gungy cake? I wonder if the French have a better word for it?

My logic is that if I can spend £220 on my bike plus the wine, then I can spend £1 on a cake. But what about my narcissism – my waistline? It's down at the moment – I can get my jeans on.

Now that I've got a new book you might find that I use the paragraph a lot more. I felt uncomfortable trying to preserve space and not start new paragraphs.

***

Right. This is the first. Letters to my friends. This is to Urline. The reason for this is a desire to write a letter to a person who might share my current interest. A second reason is to worry less about rejection and worry more about creating better relationships.

First, I'd like to summarise Stevenson's essay on the 'Truth of Intercourse'.[5] It's about relationships but when you asked me to tell you what it said, I was stuck. All I knew was that it said things that made sense to me and broke the subject into smaller parts that enabled me to understand it better.

***

The maxim that it is easy to tell the truth but hard to tell a lie is wrong.

Truth is difficult to discover and difficult to express. Whilst this is so with material measurement, truth in human relations is more intangible and hard to seize and hard to communicate. Veracity in sentiment, truth in a relation, to your heart and your friends, never to feign or falsify emotion – that is the truth that makes love possible and mankind happy.

The art of literature is to write what you mean and to affect your reader exactly as you wish and, according to man's proficiency in that art, shall be the freedom and the fullness of this intercourse with other men. Thoughts expressed in a native tongue are more likely to be made plain because the

---

5 Stevenson, R. L. B. (1980), 'Truth of Intercourse', The Harvard Classics, Grolier Enterprises Corp, USA

most amiable qualities of his nature lie buried and have to lie fallow. The pleasure of comradeship, and the intellectual part of love, rest on these very elements of humour and pathos. If a man is unable to speak clearly, if "...we all speak in different dialects; one shall be copious and exact, another loose and meagre ... the ideal talker shall correspond and fit upon the truth of fact – not clumsily, obscuring lineaments..."

The more one can open himself more clearly to his friends, the more he can enjoy what makes life valuable – intimacy with those he loves. Conversely, a trivial, but false, phrase can insult those he is aiming to charm. As if when seeking to explain misunderstanding, or excuse a fault, and addressing an incensed mind, you assume less tact and eloquence, and offend more easily. You assume language ready-shaped for the purpose, when instead you must venture forth into zones of thought still unsurveyed, and you become a literary innovator.

Even in love there are unlovely humours, ambiguous acts and unpardonable words that spring from kind sentiments. If the injured one could read your heart he would understand and pardon. Life is not carried on by literature entirely; we have physical passions and contortions; the voice changes and speaks with unconscious inflections. Groans, tears, looks and gestures are often clearer reporters, and speak more directly to the hearts of others. Misunderstandings are averted.

Words take time and a just and patient hearing – not qualities on which we can rely. A look or gesture explains things without ambiguity and are direct expressions of the heart that have a higher authority than that not yet transmitted by speech through the unfaithful and sophisticated brain. So much so that letters are in vain for, in the purpose of intimacy, absence is a break in the relation; and for perpetuity in love, looks and bodily signals are best.

Pitiful is the case of the blind, the deaf and the ineloquent. It is a doctrine for misanthropes when the romantically dull despise physical endowments. After the possession of honour, humour and pathos few things are more desirable than a lively countenance, where looks correspond with every feeling, uncouth manners never discredit speech.

The most unfortunate are those who cultivate artful intonations and have taught their face tricks, cutting off their means of communication, and thus languish uncomforted and alone.

Many words are often necessary to convey simple meanings – many arrows from far or near, from different sides, only indicate the target we aim for. A pithy speaker can miss the point; a babbler often adds three new offences. It is a delicate affair.

The world was made before the English language, and of a different design. Language is often inadequate. Questions are often difficult to answer without a lie, e.g. "Do you forgive me?" begs the question of what is forgiveness. Lies are often told in silence. How many loves have perished for want of a man daring to betray emotion. Truth, too, may be a lie – truth to facts is not always truth to sentiment. The tenor of a conversation is made up of a part of the meaning of each separate statement. The beginning and end define but travesty the intermediate conversation.

To tell the truth is not to state the facts, but to convey a true impression. It takes two to speak the truth – one to speak and another to hear. A grain of anger or of suspicion has strange effects – the ear is ever greedy to pick up further offence. Those who have quarrelled are distant, but ever ready to break the truce.

To speak the truth there must be moral equality, otherwise misapprehensions become ingrained. Listeners note only facts which support their preconceptions. However, with chosen friends and loves the truth is easily indicated and aptly comprehended. In the closest relationship the two communicate by their presence. Love rests on a physical basis; it is a familiarity of nature's making and apart from voluntary choice.

Understanding has outrun knowledge. Each knows more than can be uttered; each lives by faith and believes by a natural compulsion. Thoughts that prompted and were conveyed in a caress would only lose if set down in words.

Yet it is in such intimacies that we must battle for the truth. Once a doubt has arisen, all the previous intimacy is but another charge against the person doubted. "What a monstrous dishonesty is this if I have been deceived so long and so completely!" Let the thought gain entrance and you plead before a deaf tribunal. You cannot appeal to the past – that is your crime! Convince the reason; alas! speciousness is but a proof against you. "If you can abuse me now, the more likely that you have abused me from the first."

For strong relationships, such moments are worth supporting. They will end well, for your advocate is in your love's heart and speaks her own language – it is she who will clear you of the charge.

For lesser intimacies, it may not be worthwhile! We are all *incompris* – all trying wrongly to do right. If they do not love us, the more fools we are to squander life on the indifferent. But the morality of the thing is excellent. It is only by trying to understand others that we can get our own hearts understood. In human feelings the most clement judge is the most successful pleader.

***

Jean Luc

Jean Luc Taxis is his name. He suggested that we write to each other. He is the receptionist at the bike shop. I took the bike back with a problem – the indicator light only works occasionally. It was a loose connection but they cannot do anything now. However, Jean Luc and I exchanged addresses. Do you think he hasn't met a Brit who gives the French wine?

This came about when he looked at the map of my 'planned' journey to Trieste. He said that Briançon was beautiful and it's on the way. So, guess where I'm going.

Maulecéne

Got waylaid in Maulecéne – maybe it's Mauceléne. Coffee is good. I'm forming a new philosophy: It's better to be one up than one down. So I keep the wine and food stocks up, get the toileting done right, make sure the bike is looked after. She's going well this morning. She knows she's got a new chain and sprocket and that I gave her some attention. The point of all this? – to have two cups of coffee whilst the going is good.

But I have this problem. No. Choice. Shall I reserve my desire for coffee until Gap? It's about eighty miles away in the mountains. Sounds too good to miss, doesn't it? Coffee in Gap at 13.30 hours.

Kisses

I fell out with the lady at the campsite this morning. I asked for money and got into difficulties with this bloody Mastercard problem. Do you know the Bank of Scotland think it's a French problem. I can't believe it. It's my fucking problem. There's going to be a major international incident. I shall write to my MP and demand that sovereignty be given up for kissing.

I've just asked the waiter why he kissed that girl three times, when in Poitiers it would have been four. With two people and two cheeks each that's four kisses – two each.

"How do you manage with three kisses?" I said.

"Tradition", he said. "Each person gets three kisses." Christ! Another woman has turned up. They kissed twice – on the lips! English?

Gap

Gap. 14.15 hours. Excellent biking country – 60-m.p.h. bends. Wondering just how far I should lean this bike over. I'm having trouble with 'lead' and 'led', 'read' and 'read' and 'lean' and 'leant'.

This square is a polyhedron. It has nine areas for drinking and eating. Each café has two areas – one outside, another in the square. I'm on the outside looking in – into the square.

I think she's German, with a very short skirt. I think she's German because she's 'strapping'.

Last night two older women turned up and set up their caravan and BMW opposite me. Two shot-putters they were but couldn't smile, and I think they were speechless. Why are the Germans so uncommunicative? I wonder if they know that they are. I think they were butch, so my luck was not in. The 'female' did smile at me this morning as we were coming out of the *sanitaire*, but probably because I was leaving.

Gap is in the mountains. I think it is in the Alps.

To get to this café I followed *Centre Ville*, and then went off into a series of 'alleyways' – that's what you'd call them in England. But an alleyway here is a shopping street about the width of a car. I don't know whether I'm supposed to ride through but I followed a series of these, looking for THE coffee bar in Gap. Then the square. Whether it's in the centre or not, I've no idea. But I'm sure it's mainly locals, and that makes it OK.

I've just given another beggar one or two francs. How come she has a gold tooth? Nobody else gave her anything.

Josephine

I've got something bothering me, and it's kind of linked to 'relationships'. I was going to write a section on each relationship that I thought I had. I still might. There has been an 'occurrence', hasn't there? Josephine.

You might think that I have ignored this occurrence. A little, maybe. I haven't adjusted to fatherhood properly yet, let alone grandfatherhood. I can make noises – clucking noises – but this isn't 'relationships'. Interestingly, I read Ben Okri and he had a paragraph on grandfathers. It was to do with words, meaning and 'beyond', remember.

"Grandfathers," he said, "will look into their grandchildren's eyes and there will be a communication. It is to do with the concern for how they will 'get across', how they will cope with life and it's uncertainties."

Well, that's nearly right. But I haven't looked Josephine in the eye. I'm not sure that I have looked Charlie and Trixie in the eye in this context. Yet I do have the concern for how they will 'get across'. I still worry about me, too. Because if I have low success I'm not a good role model. I think I need to be a good role model – not for getting things right, but for 'getting across'.

I like this idea of Okri's. I'm more concerned for Charlie than for Trixie. I sense that he is more vulnerable. I think they are both vulnerable but Trixie seems to make out OK. Charlie does too, but he seems to be more on the edge, more adventurous – only slightly – but he has this health problem, with which he copes very well. So all these things are present. R too. So Josephine is not alone in having me concerned for her. I'm not adjusted. If I am dead honest I am more concerned for Charlie and Trixie, and particularly Charlie.

Long Split Skirt

There's a young man combing an older woman's hair, or looking for fleas – getting rid of something. That's odd. Not seen that before. Would it happen in the Bentalls Centre?

I've been in France about three weeks. I've not seen a policeman, except for the odd two or three bikers.

The most interesting woman in the square right now is just opposite me in the 'centre'. I think she might be six foot six inches stood up. She has blonde-ginger hair, long. She has five bracelets on one arm. Her skirt is long, split, and red, with orange, yellow and brown flower prints. Her vest is black. On top of the vest is a crocheted waistcoat in white. I think she might be beautiful – difficult to judge. It seems that whilst the red, black and white are not blending particularly well, each item is, of itself, very attractive and 'fits' with this lady.

She's talking to Helen of Troy, who is nowhere near as interesting.

***

I've been thinking over the last few weeks that I wouldn't and shouldn't write to Urline again. I've written three and sent one.

I've felt some kind of anger about the situation. Anger about my powerlessness, about my stupidity, about the prospect.

I read a review of John Updike's latest book. He's been writing for most of his life. I compared his aptitude with mine at fifty-eight plus. What chance have I got of pulling some words together to interest both my reader and me? For example, he compares a woman taking off a tight corset with breaking into a Maine lobster to get at the meat. What kind of life must you lead to have the experience of both in order to write about them, and how do you pull them together, and how do you thread them into a story?

I'm getting close to abandoning this letter because I can't see it being so compelling to read that you should be so obliged.

My reason for writing it is to explore the capability of writing, and I reasoned that you have no obligation to read or to respond. I am using you as an audience. A therapeutic audience.

The sausages are cooking. Usually I can leave them for about an hour and they won't take any harm. I turn them now and then.

I don't want to be writing this for an hour. I want to write this between 'turns'. That way I can put in ten minutes of writing. Just had a call from Urline. Feel bad and good, but I've had a new thought. Quite positive. Supposing things are OK, but just OK. Not likely to return to how they were. Well, this might be much more than many people have experienced. I can recall it; I've recorded it. I've got prizes, for Christ's sake. What more can you ask for?

Now the next trick is not to repeat it, nor to move on. But to find out what lies in store.

Valerie Singleton may not take many risks, but yours truly is pushing at the edges.

Lesley Glaister has got edges. Mine have bristles on – kind of abrasive but wobbly at the base. I don't like using metaphors: there's always a good reason for their inaccuracy. Let's have edges, where we meet one another and explore the performance and the persona.

I have told you about Barbara Dixon. This week my passion is Joan Armatrading.

***

Cin Valley

I'll do the research some other time. You can see by now what I'm like. David Lodge rewrites his stuff. Well, I can't. And I'd like to think that I won't.

I'm sitting back to front on the bike. I've stopped eating. This should slow the process down. But that's not the objective. There are six mountains in front of me. One has snow on it; another has buildings, and those could be Crois de Toulouse – 1998 metres, on which is Fort des Salettes. OK. Mountains in front, one to the left, one to the right, and some behind me. I can't see.

A river is on the right – La Durance. Bubbling, from which a group of British kayak paddlers has emerged to set up their evening meal. I could have pitched in the woods again but I preferred to seek the sun for the evening – nearly got it right – and also for the morning. I expect it to rise between the snow-cap and the fort. Oh, I can see on the map that there's lots of forts.

Quick slurp of Côte du Rhône. Brush? No, leave the ant alone. He's reading my piece and checking my thumb. Back to writing. I just want to record the current environment. It's quite impressive, but not like Roc Suzadou though. I wonder if I could find Roc Suzadou again.

I'm here because I ride a bike.

I caught up a guy, at lights, who I thought was riding a Goldwing. But it was a Yamaha Ventura – same thing. Anyway, he said something in French and I said something in English. And we were friends.

At the next hold-up he asked if I was camping. He said he was too and that the campsite was two kilometres up the road and two kilometres from Briançon. When we arrived he wasn't camping at all – he owned the place. It's called Five Valleys but at the entrance the 'q' was missing off the *cinq*!

Briançon

Well, Jean Luc said Briançon is beautiful, and it's eight miles from the Italian border. I might go and look tonight. It depends on my writing and eating. But certainly I shall take coffee there in the morning.

I've made a mistake here. I've walked for an hour this evening and I can see that Briançon is another Carcassonne. It must have an old town preserved for the tourists. Briançon is a ski resort. It probably has a lot of old quaint villages outside. What else can all those people do that live off the tourists? I should think that I can do Briançon in about fifteen minutes tomorrow on the bike and make headway into Italy. Milan is 150 miles away. Well, Trieste can only be about 300. If I gave it a good go I could be in Trieste tomorrow night and on my way home on Saturday, well Sunday.

Briançon 'new' is pretty dead and has nothing to commend it. And I've got about forty-five minutes walking to do to get back to the tent. What was I saying about being one up? I think I can pack up tomorrow pretty quickly and be on my way much earlier than this morning. I did about 160 miles today.

I've still got some Côte du Rhône left. That's the answer, isn't it? Oh, I was going to ring Charlie and tell him I'm in the Southern Alps. It's no big deal – it might as well be Charing Cross station. That's got history too.

Italy

This is Italy. The first bar in Italy.

I've done Briançon. It's a heavily constructed fort in between all those snow-capped peaks you see photographs of. I debated about having coffee there – the last in France – but decided I was sightseeing again and so moved on. I didn't get off the bike – oh yes, I did – I looked at Pont D'Asfield: a bridge over a gorge, a boundary to the fort. They showed a picture of how it was constructed. Interesting. I wonder how many people died putting the framework up?

Anyway, first coffee in Italy. Good. With a croissant: a sweet croissant. Apricot jam, I think.

I can't communicate at all. A little French but he didn't understand my 'croissant'. I don't know how much it cost yet. It has £1.00 on the 'oven'. Perhaps they mean a thousand lira – I hope. The French bank in Briançon couldn't tell me the exchange rate for the pound sterling and the lira. I think it's about L2,200 to the pound.

It's nearly midday. I've done about ten miles. The next coffee is Turin – Torino – I hope. That's what it says on the map.

My campsite friend charged me fifty-five francs. Pretty dear, but the location was good. I set up the site for the sun in the morning. That means being in the open. So the tent was heavy with dew in the morning. But nice.

Another cable broke this morning – the choke cable – so I couldn't start the bike. Two hours getting ready and I'm sat there in all my finery, and the bike won't start. I've been cussing these Brits quietly all the time but this morning all I had to say was, "Have you got a pair of pliers, please?" So I start the bike – all of five minutes. Good stuff from being in a hell of a jam. Next, I'm next to a river. So in two minutes I have clean hands, a clean flannel, and I'm ready to go.

Here I am. Here I go.

***

This chapter is intended to be more than just an emotional outburst on my relationship with Urline. I ought to try to clarify the current situation and what the prognosis is.

So, I've a plan, well, a half-plan. A half-plan is a plan that recognises that intention and reality don't match.

My plan is to describe, explain and write about my feelings about the relationship. The plan includes the premeditation of the process which includes the circumstances – a table, a period of time; the instruments – a pen, some paper; an attitude – a purpose, but not necessarily driven emotionally.

The reduction to a half is a result of confusion, regret and the feeling that it is not possible to write this unemotionally.

I think you need to be mad to write this way. And I am sufficiently mad to do it. But you have to be around at the time: you can't pick your moment.

The moment is important because it could be quite short – a note, like a photograph, a quick snap before the moment is lost. I wonder if this will make a story? Or will it be so incoherent that there will be no flow of ideas to enable readers to settle to a theme, to connect with it and wrestle with the same issue?

Torino

I had coffee and an ice cream in Torino. It's a big place and appears to be set out in a series of big squares. Perhaps this is where the Americans got their blocks from. I was in the most expensive part of town – of interest, but I decided to leave.

Alessandria

Now I'm in Alessandria, discovering how far I have yet to go. Not Trieste today. No. Instead, I'm going for a short journey to Casteggio. It appears to be the only campsite in Northern Italy not by a lakeside. The other option is a long motorway haul to Desenzano d'Garda, where there are lots of campsites on the lakeside. This is about two hours away, I should say, by the time I've discovered how to get out of here. Casteggio is on the edge of a hilly region, so it could be OK. It also gives me the chance to maintain my routine – food, wine, wash, sleep. That means a long haul to Trieste tomorrow.

Casteggio

I'm camped on a motorway – an *autostrade*! I have a small parkland all to myself apart from two lorry drivers, who are not on the scene. I have several tables and benches nearby. I'm sat at one of them. I have 'water potable', a telephone, and one of these pay-to-enter toilet booths. I could be Thoreau in his isolation. He said he always heads west. Well, that's not literal but here, if you head west you go back to the toll booth on the motorway – it's only a hundred yards away.

I'm friendly with the guy who operates it. He gave me five 100-lira coins for the toilet. We also discussed heading west because I can't. I'm on one carriageway of the motorway that goes either to Torino, which I've just left, or Brescia, where I'm going tomorrow. But he explained with fingers that if I walked I could get my coffee in a pizzeria just down the road – heading west.

The toilet is no great shakes. They're overcharging. There's no soap and no toilet paper, though it's supposed to be there. There's a mesh floor with 600 lira underneath it. I could not get the floor up, and I don't have narrow enough fingers!

I'm supposed to be eating and drinking, not writing to you. I'm sat at my table with an expensive bottle of Dolcetto d'Alba I haven't tried yet. Sold to me by the man who sold me the salami and cheese – a speciality that is spiced by the gin berry. Is that Juniper? Sheep's cheese again – dry – but there you are: when in Rome, eat like the Piedmontese. I've also got some cans of French beer left.

It's ten past eight and two more people have arrived. I wonder if they're campers? They're not Brits. I shouldn't think there's Brits within 200 miles of this place.

I thought that instead of the bubbling torrent of a river like last night, I would have the heavy drone of this motorway. But guess what? I've got a heavy metal group practising for their concert. I should think that they're two miles away but it's my kind of music, and at about the right volume. Why do they keep stopping?

***

I've been neglecting you. You being my audience – my reader.

I've been wondering about needing emotion in order to attend to my audience. Can I do it out of courtesy? Should I make a time and a place every day, when I give you some time? Will I resolve this issue before I reach the end of my book?

Does my book have an end? If not, I need to reach some conclusion before the 'end'. Shall we accept that I will return to it soon? If I 'end' before dealing with it – c'est la vie. I think I'm going to France with a mission – to learn the language, to make a break from my current turmoil, and to 'do it'.
I need to 'do it'.

I have not been short of experiences. But I have not been driven to write. I've written to Urline.

Right now, Urline is very annoyed with me. I've done something wrong. She's not speaking to me and is cool towards me. I reacted by 'resigning' my involvement with Partheon. I was devastated. I'm fifty-eight, and still I'm, or can be, devastated. How can people treat you so? They ganged up and rejected my appeals for involvement. They must see it from a different perspective. How can an individual cause so much hurt and suffering?

I heard tonight that beetles don't suffer. We do. We have self-consciousness. If I accept the premise, I agree. The premise that hurt physically is less than hurt emotionally is still questionable. Loss of limb is not of itself so damaging as the loss of contact with other human beings that would otherwise have been the case.

I wrote to Urline recently. Said words like 'the relationship was ending' – mine, not Urline's. Said, "No more I-love-

yous." That's Annie Lennox's Medusa. *I like the song. More than that, it reflects a fundamental business issue: that the environment is changing and we have to adapt to it. I haven't quite caught the words but they are roughly describing the same thing.*

It's a privilege to have experienced this emotional upset. This emotion. This.

The major problem could be dealing with the aftermath – the cooling period, when the dismal feeling of aftermath sets in, when there is no basis for excitement. The possibility of no more "I-love-yous".

***

Moonies at 150

Because the toilet wasn't up to much I didn't wash in there. I washed feet, bum, face, everything, at the 'water potable' tap. This means when the bum's exposed the westbound traffic has a driver's-eye view from about 150 yards. Funny thing is, I was discreet. I didn't strip off, though it would have been more convenient. So I just exposed the necessary bit and washed it and covered it up again. But I'm refreshed, smelling of *verveine* again, oiled and eating and writing. What more can you want?

The little lad belonging to the couple has just jumped on my tent. He thinks it shouldn't belong here because almost everything is green. My tent is blue. Wife smiled sweetly at me.

The cheese is a disc about one inch thick. It's black. Am I supposed to eat the black part? What colour is juniper?

I haven't tried the wine yet. It's expensive, but I've got a cheap campsite.

When I left you in Alessandria (one l) I walked down a street and found the bread shop. The assistant directed me to the salami shop. I then walked on a bit and found that these towns built on this square pattern have more than one centre. So I walked from one to another. I had a beer in one and an ice cream in another. It's very confusing because the streets aren't roads – they're paved walkways – but I'm sure I'm allowed to ride my bike down them. There's no sunlight because they're too narrow.

The bread cost me about L1,000. The meat, cheese and wine cost L25,000. And this was a smart bread shop, with people willing to help me stock up for camping.

In Torino I spoke to two bike cops – one with an automatic rifle round his waist. He also looked sinister with his dark glasses. I wanted to know where the centre of town was. Well, that's a silly question, especially in Torino when it's built on this square pattern. I had my cup of coffee, and then an ice cream. Whilst the coffee is excellent, I've now got a problem. How do I get a big cup of coffee?

The pen's run dry. I'm going into serious drink mode now. They're singing in English.

Can you think of a really good reason for going to bed? Suppose there was a choice.

Hell's Angels

Let me tell you how it is. It is now 23.40 hours in Casteggio. I've told you that I'm on the wrong side of the *autostrade*, haven't I? So in order to 'get back' you've got to walk. At this moment I'm sitting at 'my' table on one of the benches. This table will seat eight. Can you come? I can see perfectly well to write. I've started again on this wine. I've got the sound of traffic on all sides. There are three sides – I'm in the middle of a triangle. One of the noises apart from the music is the sound of syncopated engines – Harley Davidson's. Hullo, I thought, I'm going to have company.

No sir. Not me.

You see, I followed the sound. Not initially. I went first for a cup of coffee at the pizzeria – which is bar cum restaurant – and then I followed these Harleys. They were turning right so I walked that way. It was about a mile, and, as the crow flies, about half a mile. What is it?

It's the Hells Angels '96 Italy at Casteggio!

They wanted L20,000 for the three days' music, camping, striptease, tattooing, bike show, and whatever Hells Angels do.

Tell me: can I have come so far and not go for at least half a day? Perhaps I'll join the Angels, or at least find out about them.

I told you that it was my kind of music. I'm dancing by myself under the light – weird. I wonder what the guys at the toll booth think? The music is so loud that I actually went to look for the loudspeaker that was put into this site!

One or two cars have come into this area, do the circuit and go out again. There's more Harleys going in. In fact this place isn't too bad for quiet and peaceful study. The noise is just background. And what noise! – rock and Harleys.

Do you know what syncopated means? Apparently the Harley Davidson engine, being a twin cylinder in a 'V' formation, fires unevenly, so there's two quick firings and a gap, which is repeated. That's syncopation. What shall I call it? – a regular unevenness. And when you get up close to a Harley, as I was at the entrance to the Angels do, the tick-over is amazingly quiet and smooth. Then once the throttle is opened a little, this fat 'splat' issues forth in syncopation. It's a very satisfying noise.

I forgot: alongside my Dolcetto d'Alba and glass is the bottle of Parker Quink Emerald – it's a nice-looking bottle – my pen case, my folder for this notebook to protect it a little, my white flannel for cleaning the pen because I've just filled it, and a torch.

I've just tried to ring Charlie but he was out – up at Julie's in Bakewell? I needed to ring someone who wouldn't ridicule me for this situation. I ought to ring Trixie or R but I rang Trixie instead. I'll ring R tomorrow. They say it's Saturday!

I've got company – somebody in one of these camper van cum caravans. He's looking for a place to park. There's oceans of space. He's moved away. I can't see him. He's behind the group of trees to my right.

How can I write something profound when all these 'occurrences' need describing? How do I convert this into something worth reading? The music doesn't allow this. It is too immediate. It's movement and rocking. No thoughts. None.

Look at that tent. Perfect angles. Sat there, blue and perfect. The Suzuki half showing behind it – blue and white, with a slight lean, parked, fitting. A group of trees behind, with some bushes. And the orange glow of the toll booth beyond that. Still. Me, part of the scene. And the music.

My visitors haven't settled yet – they're behind me and driving back round. They're back at the phone box and toilet – they'll regret that. I'm sure there's another site like mine – table and light. They're off again. They can't come back – they're on the motorway. I must be dominating the scene – I'm floodlit, you see – and I must look like Charles Dickens or something.

The only reason for me to go to the bike concert is to meet and see the people – I can hear it perfectly. There's another noise in this fairyland. They're irrigating the parts where I am not. I've just finished the wine – a whole bottle. I'm a bit chilly now. I must go to bed. But what about the music? I think the trouble with the music is that it's not good all the time. I think I'm in favour of going to Trieste. If I went to the Hells Angels it would be to impress you and others. I think I'll do my own thing. Hells Angels are yesterday's people. Let's see what I think in the morning.

***

Dear Baroux,

I am writing this in an effort to help console you in your feelings of rejection. I have no explanation, no real excuses, but I would like to put things as clearly as I can. We were friends, yes, OK. But then, even though I tried to keep things light and up front by calling you 'my mate' I always felt a little stifled, a little pressurised – you were so intense. I know it is difficult for some men to relate to women as friends i.e. I confide in them (the ones I trust) and they in me. I began to feel uncomfortable with this intensity of feeling and it began to affect my behaviour. I withdrew, and that upset you, so I tried to be friends again. This seemed to give you encouragement. I felt, feel, guilty for using you but I was trying to find a way to find some equal, friendly footing again.

You are a very unusual individual and I am never sure of the seriousness of your comments, words, etc. After a hellish weekend, the last thing I then needed was more guilt, discomfort, pressure and uncertainty. So I felt I could take no more. I am very sorry if you are hurting but sometimes I have to put my own sanity first. I enjoyed our friendship but it was too much to handle; it was encroaching on my work, and making me feel threatened. I hope everything works out OK for you.

From Urline.

I received the fax today.

I suppose it was nice to receive it. At least we were communicating. I'm not sure for how long, or if ever, but this is better than the dark, or empty, abyss of nothing.

I am going to reply; I feel I've been misunderstood. I can't put it right. But I can try to express how I see the situation. There is an objective. Friendships cannot be allowed to die if, as I believe, there is good in maintaining them.

The criticism is that I am intense. Deep or forceful feelings. Whilst I believe some of the problem lies in a lack of shared meaning for the things that I say or write, I have to agree that I have this pertinacious nature. It works well in the search for information or in the preparation of reports, but clearly it can have deleterious effects on my human relationships. It has had the opposite effect from that which I aimed to nurture: I've lost my friend.

I've just typed my précis of Stevenson's essay. It doesn't give any hope at all for the repairing of lost friendships. George Eliot didn't allow for people like me to be involved in the "delight in frank kindness and companionship between a man and a woman who have no passion to hide or confess". I understood this to mean no sexual passions at play – not passions in general. I had no sexual pretensions. Despite being older and old, I am neither mentally fit for a relationship because of my 'bonding' to R still, nor did I have the compulsion. It was an ideal Eliot position – a meeting of minds, a shared interest, a discovery in oneself of a broader life.

So what went wrong?

I don't think I was particularly well before Urline. An accident waiting to happen. Three problems was usually one too many, and I don't live a particularly stable life. My past and my future in combination might make me vulnerable to emotions outside the day-to-day. Urline must have triggered in me a repressed need for the 'Eliot' companionship, and my reaction was too 'intense' – uncomfortably intense.

For some reason I think I can see things much more clearly having typed out the letter from Urline. I understand the effect much better. Is it too late? Is that very question a flawed reaction? But friends are hard to come by despite my European trip.
I used to think in terms of 'mental searing', which remains raw and prone to small but unusual proximities but which Lesley Glaister expressed better by calling the phenomena 'edges'. Emotions, almost by definition, make people more open to express and be sensitive to feelings.

Should I have been more careful and covered this up?

Surely to God, this can't be the way? Surely we must learn to accommodate and to deal with these events in kindly, human terms despite Stevenson's analysis. To behave otherwise is to deny our uniqueness as human beings. To deny it would prevent us from experiencing the richness of life in the short time that is available to us and in a world that might never provide us with the opportunity for love.

I am not in love with Urline but possibly with the relationship and the experience. It was short-lived, and what hurts is the unlikelihood of finding something equally intense.

Reactions and counter-reactions will not allow the relationship to return. Yet, these changes do not mean we can't adapt and find new joys. This is for me, of course. But there is another person for whom joy was not the underlying reason for being part of the relationship. There was a general friendship perhaps, but the mismatch was too uncomfortable. I feel better now that I have this knowledge.

I feel exhausted and weak. Abject.

I would like to cope better but there is this discordance of being happy in one's misery. It's a longing, knowing that something so small could transform the situation. One smile, one touch.

These words don't fit easily with the need to get on with work and make the organisation successful. This is why I think we have to deal with the situation. That's not proposing that it cannot be terminated, ever.

I have this view that there are a few individuals who contravene the values and ethics of the group. Our propensity is to reject them, ostracise them and accuse them of antisocial behaviour when some criminal act is carried out.

Society, or the group, must be more compassionate and be more responsible for a fellow man. In small groups it is more important that we have the capacity of keeping the group a unity by providing a haven for those who experience difficulties. Make the group cohesive despite its disparate nature.

Trieste

Just.

Had another bad moment this morning. The bike didn't start. I thought it had blown a fuse but it hadn't. It took ten minutes to establish that – I had to unload the bike. So it was an electrical fault, which was a bit worrying. It was able to start when, by turning the handlebars, the loose connection connected. This could be serious if the engine cuts out on a corner. I've had experience of this. Perhaps it's just as well.

Two hundred and eighty miles later I'm in Trieste railway station. The man in tourist information said that the station coffee was good. I think it is. Is this the standard for the rest of time?

I had a shout-up here, which kind of spoils the occasion and my image. In Italy people decide what they want and then buy a ticket. They then exchange it for the item. When queuing for a ticket it seems people have no sense of politeness, so I decided that more of this up with I will not put. Nobody understood. Nobody took any notice.

Had another occurrence thirty minutes ago. Stopped to pay at the motorway toll and unzipped the map compartment of the tank bag. But I'd forgotten that I'd put my money in my inside pocket. Then two minutes later something hit my leg, so I stopped and walked back. No hope in hell. My second pair of glasses squashed quite flat. I'd forgotten to zip up tank bag map space. Forgetting this zip is a regular event. Why do I put valuables in there? But the station here has glasses – L20,000.

Now what am I going to do? Electrical fault and, say, 700 miles from home. I'm not sure that Trieste is the place for a weekend. But I've thought that before about towns. Shall I get the bike fixed? Shall I go to the further-away campsite? The man in tourist information said the one on the beach is better than the one in town. Still, not walking distance.

There are two tables near to me. One has two Americans talking business, and the other has a Scottish couple asking for hamburgers.

It cost an extra L900 to sit at this table. The coffee was L1,400. Good coffee but I miss the *grand café* of France, with the croissant. I had a cappuccino on the motorway. No great event, so it seems I can't get a long drink. The Italians seem to drink 'grand' cappuccinos.

I wonder how the trains get out of here. Trieste is surrounded by mountains.

I left my passport, money, glasses, maps, and 'book' on the window ledge in the gents' toilet whilst I used the WC. I have to undo lots of things – it's not a one-handed job. When I walked back to wash my hands there were people standing nearby – can you believe it? If they hadn't been honest I could have lost everything except my pen. Can you imagine losing this book?

***

If we have already started something and then decide to start something else, should we consider making the second a continuation of the first? This is something of a rhetorical question.

Life is a continuum. Projects undertaken during life may appear to be separate but I expect there to be linkages if we looked for them.

So the book continues. It needs a linkage between what has gone before, and now.

The linkage is the reason for the book. Emotions drove the act and still drive it despite things having changed, though perhaps only superficially because the focus remains Partheon. Urline has been the major factor, perhaps due to a failure in my understanding of the situation. She may be gone in reality but I still have inner conversations with both Clive and Urline.

If Partheon and Urline are no more, my reason for living has gone – but I'm still here. Do we have to distinguish between reason and purpose? A reason could be that the heart is still pumping; a purpose could be that Ma needs some care and attention. More prosaically, I want to go to Canterbury on Friday to meet some friends.

Hayton's First Law

Obelesco

Thunderstorm in Trieste. It's 6.30 in the morning and I'm busting for the toilet but I've come second – it's pissing down with rain.

I'm up a hill, in the woods, on stones, and I can barely see. They don't mess about when they have thunderstorms down here. There's a river running past my tent.

I've had lots of occurrences, and I was going to leave this campsite and leave Italy. But, despite the river, things are looking up.

It's difficult to write in retrospect when in descriptive mode because of the mood change. I'll try. You'll be interested.

This bike problem got worse. I got stuck in town for about ten minutes. It wouldn't start. Every time I got ignition I thought, good, I'm lucky again. But pressing the starter button just put the lights out and made the bike go dead.

I had to decide which campsite – the one in the town or the one on the beach. I had the feeling that from comments made by the man in tourist information, the beach site was best. With the bike problem I felt the town was necessary.

I waved at two passers-by carrying helmets. They were a thirty-ish, good-looking couple with a smattering of English. They told me where the Suzuki dealer was, and that he's shut Saturday but will be open on Monday. Relationships again.

It was then that the bike wouldn't start. I had parked at a bus stop, in the way, but outside a phone box. I rang two numbers and got nothing. Then the bike started. So I thought I'd look for another phone box. Instead I proceeded to the campsite – the bike was going OK.

The campsite is not in the town. It's about three miles out at Opicina – too far to walk into town, but here we are, arrived. Looks OK at the entrance – office and café/bar. The lady is a nice person and speaks English. Expensive though – L13,500. The Italians use the pound but I can't, can I? You might get confused. How about L13,500? What's that at L2,250 to the pound? About six pounds. She shows me to my place and it's small with just stones, no grass. She says pegs go in OK. They do – but they come out again!

So, first things first. Let's ring Assistance and then have a shower. It's about 7.00 p.m. by this time. First, I can't use the French free-phone number, so I can't ring England. The guy in the café says I have to put in coins – L1,200. So I ring 176 – the Italian International Assistance. His English is marginally better than my Italian, and my insistence on getting through to Road Rescue on a free-phone ended with him hanging up on me. Nevertheless, he gave me another number for BT – 172.01.44. First he had given me 0044 as the UK number. I discovered that the six L200 coins were returned. So my Italian operator did know that my concern was losing

50 pence each time I use the phone.

BT Chargecard couldn't tell me the Assistance free-phone number, so by this time I was wanting to leave Italy pretty damn fast. They can't queue, they have a poxy pre-purchase ticket system for buying coffee, and their phone system is illogical. So I rang Charlie. He was out, but his house-share mate helped by ringing the English Road Rescue to find the number to ring me back and tell me. This got me to Huddersfield. At last, progress. From there I eventually got Fabrienne, and she set up the usual rescue and help procedure.

I'd had two beers in the bar by this time, thinking and waiting, no food and no shower. It was looking as though I was stuck in Italy at this site till at least Tuesday, whilst somebody fixes the bike. *C'est la vie!*

Ah! But then the corkscrew! Pirsig didn't encounter corkscrews, did he? Christ! I've got rain coming in the tent, damn it.

That was nasty. I've sorted it out but I'm in among dry, damp and wet gear, and my book has got wet.

I decided to go out in my oversuit to try and re-peg the tent. The flysheet was touching the inner tent. The pegs were either loose or out because of the stones.

I've nearly managed to fix them and I've now mopped up all the water inside the tent, so I'm semi-organised and all I can do is wait. This paper's wet, so I'll stop for a bit and drink wine. It's about 8.00 a.m.!

I see no sun. But it's not raining and the trees have stopped dripping. I need sun. Half my kit is damp. Blanket, sleeping bag, jeans, shorts, jacket, pullover. And this site has little scope for me to hang things up or lay things out.

The Corkscrew Factor

Back to corkscrews. I had arranged for the bike to be attended to eventually, so I had my shower and started to get some food. Then, WHAM! Yet another problem. A real one. I was taking the cork out of my bottle of Chianti. It seemed a bit tight so thought I'd twist and pull at the same time. Well, the corkscrew broke and I was left with a spike in a one-quarter removed cork. So I went for help, back to the café, where the guy said he was busy serving customers and couldn't help – just use a screwdriver. That was a bit of useless advice, I thought, so I left in a huff.

I didn't want this problem. I wanted to eat and drink and worry about the Trieste visit.

Well, I've got a few tools with me, so the only thing to do was to see if I could grip this screw portion in a way to allow me to unscrew it. Then I could go back to the café and get him to uncork the bottle.

As it happens, my tools are under the bike saddle.

You've guessed, haven't you? Under the saddle is the battery. I thought, if there's a loose connection in my electrics I'll just check the battery.

There it was – a loose connection to the positive terminal.

Now just at that moment – I haven't finished yet – just at that moment, my neighbour walked past me with his dog. His dog, by the way, is an Alsatian. It howls when it hears a police siren. I couldn't believe it. I'm next to a howling dog.

As the neighbour walked past I said, "Hello. Do you speak English?"

"A little," he said.

"I have a problem," I said, standing by the bike. He looked kind of glum and didn't want to know. But I ran to the tent, got my bottle and showed him.

My neighbour not only has a howling dog but must be the only man on a campsite in Italy who has a pair of Mole grips – the tool every man should have, R once said. So he took out my corkscrew, lent me his own, and I was able to offer him a glass of wine. "Nice wine," he said. I left him then. It was nearly ten o'clock and I hadn't eaten, but life was a lot better. I rang up Fabrienne to tell her, and she laughed.

Pirsig didn't have corkscrews. He might have checked the battery leads though. But when?

If I could find my watch I'd tell you what the time is, but it's time for activity, to start drying my kit out. I think it's drier outside than in, so we'll get something going. I need to go to the toilet too, so some time must have passed.

Well, it was about 11.30. Now it's about 12.30 p.m. I've hung my gear over a fence. Fortunately, despite the fence being under the trees, the sun is shining through a gap. Especially for me!

I'm in the camp café. Coffee. I had a shower to get warm, and now I can see the blue sky. So, what's the plan? Try the bike. Get to town. See what it's like. At one time I had the idea that I should have a meal out. I'm in recovery mode. I need a bit of warmth and time. Time to contemplate the world. Find out what's going on.

I'm unemployed. I'm a grandfather. Neither seem real.

Christ, I like Ben Okri. How does he do it? "How to get across," he said. Well, suppose I had another problem, like unemployment, like grandfathering. Well, first we'd have to cope. Second, we need the corkscrew effect. I think I've coined a phrase. It's a perturbation, is it? If a butterfly flaps its wings in Brazil and causes a thunderstorm in Trieste, does this include the corkscrew effect or not? I had this view, before I knew about chaos theory – not understood, but knew of it – that if there was an effect somewhere, there would be some counter-effect somewhere else. My nose is dripping on this paper. Not only am I leaking from the nose, but I also had blood from the rectum yesterday and today, plus a few insect bites. Anyway, chaos. So there might be something in the theory that there's more than chaos, because there could be two butterflies cancelling one another out – but not quite. Then you add to this the corkscrew effect.

I caused a lot of my own problems: not renewing the chain, or, at least, not getting it checked; not tightening the battery lead properly; and not renewing the choke cable because it would have been a bit difficult. Quality and Pirsig.

Not only that: the tools were under the saddle; I had vaguely noticed that nudging the bike had had an effect; I was next to a man who had Mole grips; and the manager of this site was too busy to help.

I like it.

It needs a definition like Sod's law or Parkinson's law. Hayton's law says:

> *In any occurrence there will always be another unexpected occurrence that alters the outcome of the event, provided you take some action perhaps not necessarily related.*

Or

> *Whatever the problem, do something.*

Or

> *Whatever the problem, talk to someone.*

I've come to a conclusion that it's positive and not negative, and thus a counter to Sod's law:

If things can go right – keep looking.

I think this explains 'Claude' in Poitiers better than anything. I must reread Pirsig. My assumption that the clutch had snapped was wrong. I was ignorant of, or ignoring, the fact that there are other pieces of the mechanism that could have gone wrong and I could have, or should have, kept looking, like Claude did.

I was quite impressed with myself this morning. It was raining hard and water was coming through the tent in fine spray, dropping in when it had collected on the material. This was due most likely to the inner and outer sheets touching because the tent had not been set up properly. This was because the pegs were put into stones and thus were neither secure nor in the right place.

So the 'do something' on this occasion was to go out in the storm, get wet, and try and make things better. As it happened I had my oversuit in the tent, and not on the bike, in the panniers, as it is on most other occasions. Now whilst I did get wet – hair, collar, trainers and oversuit – I changed from wet to damp fairly quickly. I'm going to be OK.

The blanket and sleeping bag might dry out but even if they don't they're OK enough for me to sleep. This morning I did cover myself up with the bag. I thought my body heat would help, but I got cold. This is 'latent heat', isn't it? To dry out, to change the liquid to vapour, my heat was used, and so I got cold.

I've had two coffees here. The first was the 'ordinary' coffee – the small one. Then I had the cappuccino. The bar lady explained to me that I had the 'visitors' cappuccino. A Trieste cappuccino is much smaller: same coffee, less milk – foam. The big Trieste coffee was excellent. It tasted of coffee, which is unusual in a cappuccino. I think I'll try the small one, and then ring Trixie or Charlie.

The small Trieste cappuccino is the same price as the small coffee. When I'm rich I'm going to buy an Espresso machine and get these coffees posted to me – the Trieste and the French. You need both.

Hayton's Second Law: *Don't settle for one. Two is better.*

Is this connected to *Be one up*?

In the bar is an Australian lady who has been in Italy for several years. Her mother was Ukrainian. It's her daughter who serves at the bar and who told me about the coffee. Mother told me about petrol and that there is a kind of 'fiddle'. You need a card to get cheap petrol. No card, you pay L1800 per litre – horrendous.

She also said the border was only four or five kilometres away.

***

Next month I aim to go on holiday and visit Rome and Trieste.

Rome, for the possibility of staying at Mrs Gallucci's house, if it exists, and Trieste, because this is where coffee is imported into Europe. The ultimate cup of coffee is in prospect.

To do all these things I have to get the bike running well and reliably. And running well and reliably isn't just common sense – it's an inner need for me to bring this about. My work so far has been to make it run much better than it ever has done. And that at 80,000 miles. Yet there's more to do. I don't want the anxiety of stripping down major components of the bike, like the rear suspension, when it is functioning perfectly well. But the knowledge of a clean, perfectly lubricated component working on my behalf gives a feeling of security and an inner satisfaction – a feeling of Quality. Isn't this Zen? I may need some help. My carburettor was only three quarters completed. It has a rounded-off screw at a point of difficulty. This is the opposite of Zen. It's incomplete. It's imperfect. The reason for allowing this condition to exist is that it works satisfactorily.

We don't have to repeat Pirsig here. But it's permissible to recall that:

"A person who knows how to fix motorcycles – with Quality – is less likely to run short of friends than the one who doesn't...
...who secretly pursues these options, just for their own sake,

thus making an art out of what he is doing, he's likely to discover that he becomes a much more interesting person..."

He goes on to make the point regarding the Greek myths, saying that they imbued our culture with a tendency to do what is 'reasonable' even when it has no 'good'. Reason had been made supreme.

So I have this inner conflict: to attend to the flaw, as I see it, in the motorcycle; or subjugate it to a lesser place in the list of things to do because there is less observable value added.

All these things, from the minutiae to the grand, give life its purpose – with an end result of an unidentifiable contribution to the whole.

The reward must be the meeting of a like mind – a little self-indulgent pleasure and joy. Practice with hope.

Slovenia

So I've gone past Sezana (Sedgarnar) and I'm in a little roadside restaurant. A bit expensive by Yugoslavian standards – expensive by English standards – but here we are. The guy at the bar phoned the bank and found that my Mastercard is OK. The only thing I'm worrying about is my bike and the booze. I'm a bit cold, too. I hope it doesn't rain. My blanket and washing are out drying and sunning.

I've chosen prosciutto with olives – a kind of Parma ham, I think; followed by veal Ljubljana style – cheese and ham in a veal scallop in breadcrumbs – with salad, roast potatoes, and red wine.

They appear to have just thrown in a pâté – home-made. It's 5.40 p.m. and all I've eaten today is two peaches and half a pot of yoghurt, and, of course, two cappuccinos. I've totted up. So far: 2,300 Slovenian dollars (a little over £15) plus beer plus wine. The bread was nice, and so was the pâté.

There's a lot of ham here – sixteen or seventeen slices the size of half rashers of back bacon.

I can't see any Brits around, or Americans. No hamburgers.

A pretty girl has just walked out and back in again, perhaps to inspect the customer. I'm the only one outside.

Gostilna Grahor is a very nicely appointed restaurant. There's also a bar area with tables, where the locals are playing cards. I'm in a kind of courtyard with a wood fence – very solid-sized timber of varnished pine. There are two tables with tablecloths – I'm at one; chairs with fabric seat covers; three metal tables, white, chipped, exposing rust; cars in the car park; a hedge of vines grown high like standard roses; trees; hills; more hills and more trees; and mountains I can't see from here.

The meal is good but far too much. Where am I going to put the apple strudel and ice cream?

This red wine is purple and cold. I always thought, from experience, that purple wine was bad for hangovers. We'll see. I'm on the way to completing half a litre – two thirds of a bottle. I've got a feeling that this flask is more than half a litre – it's a mezzo litre.

The background music is good – my kind. All languages, I think, rock. I'm a bit short on terminology. I'll ask when 'he', the waiter who speaks English, comes back. He learnt English in school. He's quite good. English people, let alone foreigners, have trouble with me. He'd cracked the Mastercard problem. That's why I'm in for a big meal. I only had enough cash for a coffee and a phone call. I'm frightened of the telephone now. Too much technology for the Italian personality. Perhaps Yugoslavia, sorry, Slovenia, is different. If this place is anything to go by, it'll be the cleanest in Europe.

He's offered me today's sweet – Tiarra something. It's got cream and coffee. Can I go wrong? Should I keep my big mouth shut?

Tiramisu – an Italian sweet. A glass sweet bowl, white with something brown at the bottom centre, cream colour on top with a slight brown sprinkle, cold. It's a trifle. Three hundred dollars (£2).

I don't think this meal was a particularly good move. I feel that I should be with more people, and perhaps in Trieste. But it's only seven o'clock, so I've got time yet.

Slightly chilly, sunny, lots of cirrus around. Cirrus is usually the sign of a cold front, isn't it? Cold air on top of hot, causing moisture to condense. So if cold is on top of hot, I think it's higher pressure. Isn't that warm weather?

Sezana

Going back to the border, I thought I would try the bike – 110 m.p.h. with some more to go. Good roads, nothing about – just hills and trees. When I got to Sezana I stopped for some coffee, just because it was Sezana. So, after the coffee it seemed that half the population were coming for ice cream. So I had a vanilla cone – 600 dollars. At 150 to the pound that's about £4, isn't it? Anyway, it's good ice cream in Slovenia. So I had a chocolate ice cream. Next, I bought some petrol and used up all my money. Well, I bought some oil as well. I had to use a few lire – don't ask how many. When it gets into thousands, it's difficult to know whether you've lost twenty quid or not. The petrol attendant then came out and asked if I would buy some old English pound notes and five-pound notes. I felt a bit dubious because I don't know if the bank would honour them. I feel rotten for refusing. Damn – I let the nation down.

***

I've been depressed for three or four weeks. Well, since Christmas really. I've had two sets of pills – one being Prozac – but they didn't make much difference, but how do you know?

Now I've had a major 'traumatic' – Urline has turned on me and Partheon have got rid of me. I did two fairly major pieces of work – the last throes of a dying man. Urline was cool. I couldn't cope with that climate so I set in motion my departure. I was wrong. I should not have been so precipitate.

They don't comprehend what distress this whole saga has caused me. I don't understand what I've done, and I don't understand how people can treat one another so badly.

This depression has had the effect of making me tearful and totally abject. Whilst I can put on a performance I don't know how others perceive it, or me. I can also see that 'pulling myself together' is an option. I don't want to. I haven't got the energy. I have displacement activities. I can fix the bike – I've done a good job on the carburettor. I've also revisited Pirsig – Zen and the Art of Motorcycle Maintenance – to refresh my mind on his concept of Quality.

It's my relationship with people that's the problem. A regular job that isn't Partheon seems out of the question. It won't have the same consuming passion. The prospect of meeting people who can become close seems remote. So I foresee a bleak future.

I wanted to see the shrink but available appointments clashed with my promise to Alan to accompany him to the West Country. I really want to see this lady shrink. I think she's a psychiatrist but I'm unsure. I want to be confirmed ill. I need that before I can get better. But I've promised the world I'm going on holiday. That's going to delay my confirmation, sod it.

I'm disappointed I haven't kept my writing up. I haven't had the 'need'. This session is rather exploratory. Trying to find out what's there once in the situation of having pen with paper.

My pen, by the way, is a 'special' – an expensive gift to myself to make my writing an occasion. I'm afraid of regularity, writing by rote and without passion. There's no Urline to tear at the edges – my edges.

Rosie's read my writings. She suggests I've got a style that's worth pursuing. This was based on my love letter, but I can't write like that every day. It's got to be like this. Rosie's lent me David Lodge's Therapy, *and he writes like this. I'm sure this is better, but unfortunately this doesn't have a story.*

Perhaps when I get on the bike, and head east, I can find a thread to give it some continuity. That's one of the reasons for returning to Pirsig. Combine philosophy with a bike trip. Still, I haven't started yet. Without a start I can't fail, can I?

I don't think I know enough. How can I explore human relationships when I've only got my own personal experience to relate? Don't I need some good theory and propositions from the social scientist first in order to stop my reinventing the wheel?

Partheon, you see, have lacked integrity and sincerity, in my opinion. It's these factors that could be worth exploring. I tried an integrity search on the Internet but I only got religion. Perhaps I should try sincerity.

Nothing! But I did get into relationships. The effect of that was to effectively stop me planning to tell Partheon they lack integrity and sincerity, because it won't work. I could rephrase it. I can say that I still have faith in them.

I wonder how my relationships compare with other people's. In number there's R, my ex; Sally; Natalie; Urline; Rosie; Sheila; Julia perhaps. That's seven females. Alan, Mark, Tony, Chris, Cathal – I'm struggling – Will, and some distant friends. Six males, at most, and immediate male friends could be just two. Accuracy is not important here, especially as the number changes over time.

Closeness is different. Easier to identify but difficult to be open about. I confide in Sally, Natalie and Rosie. Is it because they're female? I think it's because there's a warmth in the friendship that doesn't exist in the others, and perhaps females can give a bit more compassion. Well, I perceive them as having that capacity. On the other hand a male – Alan, for instance – can listen and empathise, but doesn't bolster the ego.

The problem with this writing is that it is rational and thoughtful. There's no emotion in it. I need to find some. Can it just be turned on? Perhaps we could again refer to Pirsig, who proposed that reason should be subservient to Quality: doing something good cascades down or along to others such that its benefits are spread wider.

If I explore these relationships of the 'good' and its 'benefits', the exploration has to be much more than a description. It needs to capture the significance of an act in relation to a resulting attribute or consequence.

I mentioned this to R yesterday but as it was in connection with Charlie the discussion soon degenerated and alluded to my fickleness. He's not on the list. Why should I have excluded my son from the list of males – and Trixie from the list of females? It's possible that these are the most important relationships. Perhaps they're special and need special treatment.

Offspring are close, but for some reason I am reluctant to fully disclose thoughts, to share feelings. I did get close with Trixie at Christmas though, when I was getting uptight about Urline. There is love between us but the problem is that I have a different role. I'm not fully me. Or is it the other way round? I am exactly me but without the performances yet with the imposed role of the medicine man – a mythical figure who has answers and no questions (John Bowle's Western Political Thought *probes human relationships from an atavistic perspective).*

Perhaps it's the reluctance to get close that impels me to try and get close to another person. This is where wives fit. But it doesn't have to be wives only. Another person can get close too. Not as close perhaps, but sufficiently close for them to become part of your life – a needed part. Part of the Gestalt.

So what's missing now? Why am I so depressed? Why do I need to belong to this other group? Not instead of, but as well. And is there a sneaking feeling that one is more important than the other? And perhaps it's the wrong one?

How does one form such an important part? Partheon isn't a person. It's distorted by Urline being part. But I was attached to Partheon before Urline became important. Partheon was the vehicle through which I could reach fulfilment – self-actualise – and these opportunities don't occur very often, if ever.

So perhaps with relationships it's not what the other person brings, it's what that other person enables you to do or express. Empathy and congruence enable another person to behave freely and explore their own personality. By so doing, they can develop more of their potential.

How come this doesn't happen with your own kids?

***

Istanbul – Not Quite, but Nearly

After exploring Slovenia I decided it was time I saw Trieste. I got there about 8.30–9.00, and I just mooched around on the bike – looked at the docks and suchlike. I saw a group of lorry drivers in the lunch area so I stopped and asked the best route to England. They said Milan, Questo, Paris. Where the hell Questo is, I don't know – I haven't looked at the map.

These guys were Turkish, from Istanbul. When we got chatting, with signs and nods, one of them offered me some raki. That was good. Because I was off the bike by this time, I had walked over to where they were sitting and asked what it was they were eating. It's amazing what you can do with about five words. So he gave me a forkful of what was omelette plus some salad that included chilli. So, we shared forks and glasses.

Then another was prompted into asking for a ride so I took him round the lorry park on the pillion. There must be another law somewhere about relationships but I don't know where to start. Is it genuineness, or congruence, or both? Are they the same anyway?

Then I went to the 'jetty' and bought another ice cream. Stopped off at what I thought was a biker's bar but it was 100 to 200 people watching Germany play Czechoslovakia for the European Championship. The phone box was occupied and I couldn't phone Trixie, so I thought I'd go back to the camp and phone from there.

Here I am, in the bar, into my second bottle of wine – the first in Slovenia!. That must make about ten glasses today. But the phones are still down after the storm. I'm not doing my grandfathering very well.

Looks like throwing-out time. No it's not – not until eleven o'clock.

Well, I'm off tomorrow. I need to know if I can do the Alps in one day.

If so, it's Austria, Germany. If not, it's what the Turk told me – Milan, France. For some reason I am reluctant to go through Germany. Probably because I think a third unfamiliar language might cause me difficulty if I want to get home reasonably quickly. Milan to the Simplon Pass is good but I've done it once. If it doesn't matter what route I take in terms of days I'd like to do the Austria–German trip. I can put up with the money problem. I've managed so far, and I do have some marks. I also think the Germans, as a nation, are more likely to speak English. Right, to bed. Let's go home.

Villa Solintyes.

Don't let the waitress read this. She's beautiful. She's nice. She's everything you'd expect an Austrian waitress to be. Dressed in red and white and swirling, and all that 'German' girls wear on occasions. She speaks beautiful English. She calls veal 'weel', but never mind.

What shouldn't she read?

It's been a fucking awful day. A piss-awful day.

But I'm here. Can you believe it? It's the 'Corkscrew Factor'.

I got up early, ready to buy coffee to take home, and to buy postcards to send home. But I had to wait until ten to get out of the campsite. That was no problem. I had the runs. So I had to hang about to make sure I was motorcycle-fit.

Well, I had three coffees – a large cappuccino, a small cappuccino, and an espresso – plus an Italian doughnut with jam, then a kind of croissant with cream. It had rained but was clear. Of course, my fucking prediction about cirrus was the opposite of the truth.

I've been in the Alps, doing hairpins in torrential rain. Never mind 'wet bum'. How about wet gloves? On and off fifty thousand times to pay:
1) tolls for the motorway, and
2) a speeding fine in Austria – a whole 500 schillings. I think that's about thirty quid.

I had just stopped. Wait a minute! How about the time I slid? Two wheels on the hairpin. How about the first ten minutes? I reach a blue sign indicating Udine, which is where I want to go, then don't take the blue sign to Vela something, which meant I missed Udine. Another balls-up –

Italians navigate by colours. Having missed the blue, I end up on the green. Then have to pay God knows how much for the toll for the *autostrade*, which is green. That's not British, is it?

Never mind, I say. I want to make progress. I'm going home.

You see, the alternative was to go to Milan on the *autostrade* and go across the Alps at Simplon. I've done it before, in the opposite direction, when I went to Stresa for the seminar. North to Udine was the choice to get into the Alps. West was the Milan route.

Then at Tolemezzo, I think, was the town to turn left, or west, for the country road towards Bozan. Well, I chickened out on that and went on the quicker, main, road to Austria, due north. Don't look; I might be wrong. Anyway, it started to rain, so I kitted up.

Too early, I thought. It'll just be dull. Balls. It rained for hours.

I set off at eleven, not knowing if it was going to take two or three days to get home through the Alps with all this good riding country. I end up saying, "Can I do it in one day? Do without sleep? Let's get home and out of here."

This was ten miles per hour on the bends, and forty to sixty on the straights, with traffic going and coming.

I had this slide and concluded that this 'riding on the edge' was, for me, quite risky. But I needed to keep the average speed up.

I also had this problem: if my credit cards don't work, have I got enough cash? Particularly when I'm headed for Hungary. Well, I wasn't. I ended up at the Italian-Austrian border. And, of course, had coffee.

Tell me the truth. Is '*a* coffee' different to 'coffee'? 'Coffee' is an occasion – with friends. 'A coffee' is a cup of coffee – a bit naff. I'm concerned about this, because my mother says 'a coffee'. I'm sure I would have normally said, "Let's have coffee." There's a bit more class about that!!

Having done that border I was going to cross the same border again but the other way round. I had lira, you see, which meant I could buy petrol. This was at Wittenbach, or something like it.

Well, it was raining so hard, I was forming the idea that this mountain trip was a mistake. Let's find an *autostrade*, and so I changed routes. Let's go to Innsbruck, not Bozan. Where the hell is Innsbruck? It's in Austria. I got to the border at Brennen. I spoke to a beautiful lady at the crossing. She gave me fifty marks for my lira.

So I crossed the border. I thought, I've got to make progress. I've done 150 to 200 miles and it's rained, so let's oil the chain and check the oil, so I don't worry if I go faster.

You understand that by this time I'm wet, especially my gloves. Every stop demands a procedure; some more than others. Gloves and overgloves. Tank bag and cover. Oversuit zip and jacket zip. God, it's a pain. Particularly those gloves. It's a wrestling match to get the oversuit sleeves over the gloves and then to get the overgloves over everything. That's to stop water running down my sleeves and straight into the gloves.

I must have stopped a million times. Pay the toll, change the money, buy some petrol. Then ride off and find I'm cold. Why? I haven't done my helmet up. I haven't done my jacket or oversuit up. Stop. Put it right. Ride off. Then, oh God, where am I going? So, stop, off with the gloves, out with the map, find the location – in the rain, never mind – fold the map, stick it back in a crumpled heap.

Then, going well, in the traffic, 80 to 90 m.p.h., fucking *gendarmerie*. Caught doing 85 to 90 in a 60-m.p.h. area. I'm being fined, so off with the gloves, search in the tank bag for passport, can't find it, search for money, can't find any. Officer spots traveller's cheque and settles for that. This takes about three quarters of an hour. Then he has the view that my earplugs are dangerous. "Can't hear the traffic," he says. Fuck. Thirty quid. I'm still in trouble. Why haven't I got my driving licence and vehicle registration certificate? "They're not necessary, officer."

Don't be an arsehole, he thinks. "That is 500 schillings, and don't do it again," he says. This makes my day.

Let's drive to Calais, even if it takes all night. I can catch snatches of sleep at cafés and things. Let's go for it.

Well, let's go for it, with gloves on and off, to check the direction. So we go for Strasbourg. Then it's petrol time. Running out. For Christ's sake, I can do without the worry of running out. But we find a town and get off the *autostrade*, and find the petrol station. The Mastercard doesn't work, does it? I'm getting totally pissed off with this credit card problem. But the attendant keys in the number and it works so, thank Christ, I'm up and away, petrol, oil and chain OK.

So we're off to Calais, via Strasbourg. How far? God only knows. Then

I see a camp sign. No, I thought, it's too wet. But after a time the idea takes hold. It's stopped raining. Perhaps I should camp for a fiver and spend money on food.

I could just go to a hotel. Or I could have a slap-up meal and continue to ride to Calais.

I see two more camping signs, and turn off.

***

Perhaps we are too often driven by process rather than content. I've sat down, more concerned with pen and paper and context, with nothing to say.

Many writers, so I believe, write by rote – a set period at a set time each day. But you can't turn passion on like that, can you? Or does passion last for months, or even indefinitely, so that it's like turning a tap to allow more to come out?

That might not be a bad thought. Ride for a period to the next table top and allow the urge to write to be freely expressed.

You need to have something to say. Scraping around in the mind for comment isn't going to interest many people.

Pirsig tied his commentary to the bike and explored the concept of Quality. I think that if I was going to explore a concept it would have to be 'relationships'. Not the ephemeral kind, but the genuine feeling of companionship without judgement.

There seemed to be little problem with this in my youth. Relationships developed and were accepted as permanent, without any judgement of any kind. Whilst they have held throughout life it is odd that, as we have grown older, and lived further apart without seeing each other for long periods, the relationship still exists. But it has lost its sense of pleasure in companionship.

New friends have assumed much greater importance, though

there is much less daily involvement. We all have separate lives. But that is only my perception. It may be specific to me, and that my capacity to form friendships is waning with age.

***

Innerbraz, Austria

It must be the best site in Europe. I'm showered and beautiful. Now, I'm at the end of Villa Solintyes: wine, beer, ice cream and coffee. Don't ask the price. I'm just pleased to be dry, warm and fed, and happy to be here writing to you – if you can read it, that is!!

What's this Corkscrew Factor then? It's the unexpected: police, camping site, drink, ready for bed.

When I finished my meal I went to the bar to have a 'local' drink – Schnapps – and I met four Dutch people. Bruer, his son Tjitti, Karim and her husband Richard They all spoke English and we got on quite well and each made a contribution to my journal:

Prettige reis nog. Tjitte Ackerman.

Strange way off meeting some person dat's one off the kind, with love from the boys.
Bruer Akkerman
Laan V. Vollenhove 1443 3706 E.W. Zeist

Have a nice journey, drive carefully, and maybe we see you next year in England! We met at Innerbraz. dd 1/7/96 – Austria
Karim from Holland.
Meby you have next holiday more lucky with your dutch this year (suskiê).
(Goldwing) 1200.Richard from Holland
Prokofseustreet 186 1323 Almere Holland.
Tjitte is seventeen, Bruer is divorced. Karim rides a Honda something, but it's a custom bike. Richard rides a 1984 Goldwing, and wears clogs.

It's morning. I've been back to the 'facilities'. They're centrally heated! Pristine and tiled. Water too hot and needs cold. My salopets are dry. My gloves would have been too if I'd realised there were radiators. So. What do you think? It wasn't such a bad day. The policeman who wished me a good journey might have influenced that. He delayed my progress by half an hour, pissed me off, and put me in the frame of mind that getting to Calais was now remote, hence the thought of camping.

Now that I've looked at the map, I'm a huge distance from Calais. I'm at Innerbraz, halfway between Innsbruck and Zurich. It looks like more than a day's riding to Calais. I'm hanging about a bit – the tent is wet but not bad. Perhaps I'd better pack up before it rains. It's a bit overcast but not threatening.

I was drunk last night. Bruer bought me another Schnapps and then I had a beer in his tent. I don't remember going to sleep. I woke at five for the toilet, then again at eight. Showered again because it's nice, and came into the hotel for a coffee. The site is a field, well, parkland, at the back of the hotel – or is it a restaurant?

I'm reluctant to go, but I need to make progress. Progress is a phrase used by the Institute of Advanced Motorists. They discuss 'progress' in the form of driving close to the speed limits and overtaking where possible, not holding people up, and purposefully 'making progress'.

Go and see my Dutch friends first.

Schaffhausen

I'd better not stop; I'm supposed to be making progress. I've stopped for money in order to get petrol. Several garages didn't take Mastercard, so I can't afford a cock-up. So having stopped for money, I've also stopped in a bar. Looks like a bit of a locals' bar. So I have what the natives are having – a glass of wine.

One of the locals stopped to talk to me and tell me about the journey to Freiburg. I think he's mixed it up with another road. Never mind; I seem to be accepted as one of the locals. He says about three hours. I'm not making sufficient progress. It's further than I thought – ninety miles. It's through the Black Forest so I'd better go and see it. As I go out I say goodbye to no one in particular, but almost everyone replies. I think everyone, including me, was self-conscious. The farewell broke the ice, and it gave a warm feeling.

It's quite cold. I have my oversuit on to keep the cold out. I really need my pullover on too – full winter kit.

Kayserberg, France

I've done 230 miles today. A bit short of target and yesterday's 320, but I might be within reach of Calais tomorrow. Trouble is, it will be a long way – it's all travelling. No hanging about in coffee bars. Or *charcuteries*. I would like to take some cheese back to England. Wine is bulky. I think I can buy reasonable salami and sausage back home but cheese – that is more difficult.

Kayserberg is an interesting village. I've got a feeling it's Alsace. If it is, that could explain the German look about the architecture, and the geraniums in the window boxes. It's very pretty and quaint, and well kept. It's spoilt by the lack of local people. No natives. No mopeds. No noise. It's all tourists – upper class tourists plus the retired. That's what the campsite is – full of retired caravaners.

I've missed the shops, so I've only got my Italian food and two cans of beer. Hard done by, aren't I? The bread seems OK. I don't know. I'm not there. I'm in a hotel cum restaurant drinking beer and wine. The wine is sixteen francs. That's a bit dear, isn't it? *Trop cher*. But it's good. Perhaps that explains it. I've got to get back before ten – no noise, and the gates are shut.

That campsite in Austria: you've got to go. The hotel, restaurant, was so good. They were nice, everybody, all dressed traditionally. And the veal, salad and the ice cream were excellent. But – you've guessed already – the coffee is not so good. It looks good, it has a nice dense *crema*, but the coffee is too weak. Or should I say mild?. They serve cream separately in a little jug. 'Little jug' is smaller than 'small jug', isn't it? It contained about a tablespoonful. Perhaps I should put the cream in the coffee. Cream spoils good coffee, I think, but in weak coffee there might be an improvement. That's nonsense, isn't it? Cream with good coffee is nice. Like the Italians' cappuccino. I shall miss that. I must get up to Waterloo Station and see what their coffee is like – cappuccino, I mean.

I ordered a red wine, Fr8.50 – half the price of the white. It makes the point of how good the white was. If I drink any more I'm going to eat the food here. No tourists – I think they're people who know this place.

Perhaps on my last couple of days I can justify it. What I mean by that is that, although I could live in a tent knocking round Europe, this trip could well be my last. I'm not back yet. I've had a good trip, but I've got good vibes about this restaurant. Let's increase the overdraft – no, that's not true – let's use the temporary overdraft, and think about it later. I've forgotten my glasses and the light is not good, so I'll write slowly. But sometimes that is not possible.

I had an 'occurrence' in Schaffhausen. I got fifty Swiss francs out of the machine – about twenty pounds. This was for petrol plus emergencies. I went into the bar where I wrote to you, remember? Well, the bill, I thought, was two Swiss francs but she charged eight. I felt annoyed. I was done. But my maths was probably at fault and I didn't count my change properly.

Now, in Kayserberg, I gave the waiter here 200 francs and he gave me change for 250 francs. Because I've decided to eat, I've been back to the campsite to check where to put the bike if they have shut the gate. I won't get back before ten, which meant I had to go and come back on the bike. The reason I couldn't walk back is that my order had to be made before 9.15.

On my return I said words, in English, to the effect that earlier that day I had been given too much change. I had been rather diffident to mention it for some reason. Anyway my first waiter came back and checked and agreed he'd given me fifty francs too much. So I now have a Tokay on the house. It's the white wine and it's excellent. Remember: Tokay.

My meal is excellent. First, the wine is Pinot Noir. Now, if you've read this far and noted that wine, you've gained. This is Alsace. My white is Tokay, or Pinot Grey – or whatever the French is for Grey. There's a Pinot Blanc. But Pinot Noir – or black – is really nice. It's different, more flowery. It looks like Rosé.

My meal was *jambon* something. Gammon slices in a sauce. The gammon was a cross between ham and smoked bacon. The sauce was not mushroom but that colour, and had other flavours. The hors d'oeuvre was salad and sausage. The rice was like basmati. Super.

Now I'm going to have ice cream – coffee and vanilla. Everything is a new taste experience – the ice cream is very icy, not creamy. Very refreshing. Nice.

This Tokay gets better.

Now I'll ask for coffee. Aren't you glad you persuaded me to eat here? I could hear you saying, "Go on; go for it. It's your last chance!"

Trouble is, this could be just self-gratification. Whilst that is true, there is something else. I'm not sure what. Will you get any satisfaction from hearing about my experience, my extravagance?

But without having the experience, how will we ever know? So, I'm glad I'm here.

Now I'm going to ring my family.

Bruer, the 'Dutch father', has asked me to write to him. That's good, isn't it? – as long as I do. His son is called Tjitte, pronounced Shitter.

Just spoken to the people at the next table. They're Dutch. They say this place isn't exceptional – there are a lot of good restaurants in Alsace – but the wine is good.

The coffee was good – strong and smooth. A little different. I must find another word to describe coffee that is good, strong, but not smooth. Rich.

Going Home Blues

There is something different about going back. There's a loss for some reason. I'm not free. You need freedom to stop and go to the unplanned-for place en route. I have this feeling that I shouldn't be here drinking this coffee. It's not on the agenda for making Calais tonight.

Going back ought to be part of the holiday or trip. Prepared for the unexpected – good things, I mean – change direction. Right now there is only one direction. Anyway, this is the plan:

1) Go over to Cavean Rocher across the street (they sell wine) and check the prices – I've already been to the supermarket – and then try another shop further down the street. If I'm not convinced, then as a fall-back position, go back to the supermarket.
2) Buy postcards of *cuisine d'Alsace*.
3) Buy petrol at the supermarket, ride for 100 miles and see what the time is, and replan – the processual approach.
4) Ring my mother to let her know what the plan is. There's a sub-plan: go to the north of Angers and find that bar where the coffee is good.

When I was in the civil service working, if you stayed away long enough the work would disappear. It would all be too late or unimportant. I've got this dreadful feeling that I'm riding back to facing a shitheap of paper and chores. I'll abandon that thought for a bit.

It seems to me that Partheon are the only friends I haven't got. That's another pain in the butt.

I haven't taken my 'happy' pills for days. I couldn't find them this morning. Without the Hopes I don't need them. Pinot Noir is better. But the Hopes are a kind of necessity. Newton's third law of thermodynamics: you can't win, you can't break even, but you have to stay in the game.

An Indian soil scientist in Cambridge – I can't think of his name right now – told me that this law was the fact that everything will revert back to its natural state: entropy. For example, leave a bottle of perfume in a sealed cabinet, and in time the cabinet will be evenly filled with the mixture of perfume and air. I'm not too sure if the glass would eventually be transformed. It sounds like you can't avoid the inevitable.

It's 11.30. Time for executing the plan.

11.32. Plan modified. I asked the waitress where I should buy the local wine. She and her colleague described the way to Bernard Haas, down here on the right. Tell him I came from Restaurant Le Capucin. I'm parked outside a church. There's two girls – women, should I say? – playing the violin: Mozart, Haydn, whatever. They're surrounded by people clad in coloured shorts and video cameras.

OK. Done Bernard Haas. A little taste, shook his hand, two bottles packed. Hope now the bottles don't break my glasses. Should I change panniers? I think so. Sods law! It is now 12.00.

Metz

Not such a great place. But I've made that mistake of premature judgement before. Towns need to be discovered.

A hundred and twenty miles so far. No croissants, so I haven't eaten yet. This is just a bar. I must discover the difference between a bar, a café and a restaurant.

I'm working up to eating out again. The other idea was to find a farmhouse and stay the night. I don't know the French for bed and breakfast. In fact, I've not seen the word *pension* at all.

This is a two-kiss area.

This is good biking country if you want to make progress. It's mostly 70 to 80 m.p.h., with some good bends. That is about all you can say for it. Since Ludeville, near Nancy, the towns and villages have been dull and the countryside is rolling hills, big fields, and grain country.

In a café bar. The table next to me has six people and a baby. There is one small cup of coffee only, and one of the group is eating a takeaway Chinese they have just bought from across the 'street'. This is a long, funnel-shaped square, and I'm at the narrow end.

It's a long time since I've had salami, cheese and wine. That would be an attractive proposition right now.

Charlesville Mezieres

Just a quick write whilst there's light. I'll recount more fully tomorrow. We'll try that.

Everything normal until Charlesville Mezieres. Need to find 'my' Youth Hostel. No signs. Ask taxi drivers at the station. They laugh, and show me the way on the town map. When I get there, it's closed.

Back to plan B. Go for the campsite that I had seen the sign for. Get in. Quickest pitching of tent this trip. Ask a German couple, in Yiddish, about shops – nobody understands anybody. But at 7.00 p.m. (220 miles today, by the way) it's close to shop closing time, so I need to erect the tent in case it rains – it's been trying to all afternoon – and get away to the shop for food. I know I've got enough food, but the wine... I need wine.

So, it's jeans and sweatshirt, on the bike, and off to the shop. Fuck me. Could I find the town? Could I hell. Lost in the back streets. I had turned right, looking for the shop, instead of going straight on. Then I see a sign for Carrefour, the supermarket, on the route to Le Retoux. Well, Le Retoux may as well be on the moon.

All signs are for Paris, Toulouse, Morocco – all these bloody places – but not Retoux. Well, it's beginning to drizzle by this time.

Then, chancing my luck with a left turn, I end up on a motorway access. Oh Christ: rain and sweatshirt and jeans.

So, I set off on the motorway and then first exit to try to find my way back through more back streets.

I have some luck but, what to do? Find a tree, a bus shelter? A bar would be OK. But... nothing. Then these bloody traffic lights. French traffic lights have this interminable time between changes. I've been very near to tears tonight. Fucking rain, fucking traffic lights and no bloody shops.

Then! Then! The main street. I know it well. I've already done it twice when looking for the Youth Hostel.

Would you believe it? A grocer in the main street of the town. It's open. Well, she said it was but she was washing the floor. So, have cheese, wine, yoghurt, peaches; and I'm a happy dude. No *saucisson* though. The rain's getting harder. I go back.

Then. Then. A *charcuterie*. Open. So, "Always be one up." I stop and go in. We have a weird conversation. I end up with *Fromage du Tête* – I had *Fromage du Tête* at Kayserberg, and it was delicious – and some of the man's own pâté. I ask him what time he closes. He says 7.30. By this time it's 8.10 so I suggest he had stayed open for me. "*Il pleut,*" he said. Another friend. They're fantastic, the French.

Back at the tent. Everybody on site is hatched down due to the rain.

Baroux is not too wet. Body heat and frustration keep the shirt and jeans reasonable. Only wet bum. Sitting on wet saddles, you see.

I think, let's have a shower. I need to smell my *verveine*.

So, off to the shower despite the rain. Come back – nearly back to normal. You know, clean, dry and oiled.

So I decide to – oh, by the way, my new habit is to 'take beer' in the shower. Warm shower, nice soap, French beer – in a glass. Perfect. I took up this idea in Austria. So good were the facilities, where else would you take beer? Anyway, back at the tent, and ready to eat. Fuck me – the Corkscrew Factor! Remember I broke my corkscrew? Remember we made laws? Remember we took a great leap forward in understanding the world? *Mais je ne se rappelle pas mon fucking tire-bouchon; il est briser.* Oh, woe!

But it's alright now. The camp commandant just happened, well...

I'd thought I'd start writing again – it'll slow the pace of eating and drinking. I've got oceans of food, perhaps mountains, with oceans of drink. I had asked the lady what the locals drink – you know: *je vouderais du vin* and wave my arms about saying "Charlesville". She looked blank at 'Charlesville', but she pointed to a bottle at Fr10.50. When I get it home it's OK wine. I find it's from Provence de L'Herault. At Fr10.50, perhaps that is what they do drink around here. Anyway, back to my *fromage* and *saucisson*.

I've got some good stuff here. The only thing missing is a German salad. German mixed salad is really good. Really good. I'm going to learn how to do it.

There's a noise going on here which I can't believe the town would put up with. First I thought it was a train going over the points or joins. Then I thought it was a very long train. Next, because about twenty minutes had passed, I thought it was army gunfire. Now I think it's an event with drums. I can't really believe it. There is some cheering going on as well but I don't know if it is the same location. Anyway, it's a lot of banging, like a train going over points, or a steam hammer making tank parts. Gunfire and drums.

Well, here I am, sitting in the campsite light – darkish – quietly pissed. I've just thrown the bottle out. The drumming has stopped. I've eaten all I can – some great stuff – and I could just do what I said I usually do. Just lie back and go to sleep.

I don't think that my housekeeping is quite in order for that and, besides, I still have some wine in my glass. It's 10.30. The drumming has stopped. I ought to drink water but I can't be bothered. I'm going to organise for bed.

My camping neighbours have returned. They sound young. The nearest are forty- to fifty-year-old men with younger women and new motorbikes. Do you think that there is a connection? One woman is a pillion. The other has her own motorbike. Germans, of course. No, maybe Dutch – they were friendly.

I shall tidy round, take my trousers off, and go to bed.

Well, I woke at 6.00, and went to the toilet and showered. It was raining. I'd kind of made a decision to stay up then because of the rain. There was no prospect of it stopping. I thought I'd start packing.

I couldn't quite see how I could pack everything up and get the tent down in the rain and stay dry. I got all my kit on – leathers and oversuit – having done the panniers, blankets and clothes, and just started. I've done it so quickly. The tent was easier than I thought. First, when the outer tent – is that the flysheet? – is wet, it rolls very tightly. Underneath the ground sheet was dry, so I ended up on the road at 8.00.

Cambrai

Here I am, in Cambrai. Coffee, and a couple of croissants.

When in Metz they taught me how to say croissant. I said KWOSON.

This should be KRWOSO. Because it was just a bar, they didn't serve food so perhaps my request for KWOSON was not expected and therefore not understood. I would have thought it was close enough.

Last night I said I would rewrite my 'drama'. I remember that. I don't usually read what I have written but I have got the feeling that it was good enough. I mean by that, that I won't be able to add or improve anything.

I would like to reflect on the Corkscrew Factor though. I think the Corkscrew Factor tends to be a good outcome influenced by unconnected events. I'm not sure that it's a 'Do something, no matter what', but it could be just that. Nor do I believe it's the counter to 'Don't stay home and mope about it'.

There needs to be an association somewhere – a tenuous link. But opening a bottle of wine is far removed from electrical faults on motorbikes.

Pirsig's book is quite long, and I don't know where to find the reference. I think he said somewhere that Quality means to persist, to think round the problem, don't be put off. I once lost a nut when I was doing some do-it-yourself on the Citroen I once had. It was in an impossible position. I couldn't get at it, and without it I was stuck. Somehow I did do it, which kind of reinforced my understanding of Pirsig's 'Quality'. Something beyond reason. Linked too to Okri's 'How do you get across?'

There were two beautiful girls in this bar, both black. Well, one black, one dusky. 'Dusky' had her hair drawn back 'Spanish' style. 'Black' had her hair in tight, small plaits. That hairstyle is impressive. They were behind a plant and I couldn't see very well. I thought I would keep an eye on them to see them more clearly if they got up to leave. Well, I missed them.

It seems that two *grand cafés* puts my caffeine level right – I feel very contented. I'd like to go back to the *confectionerie* where I bought the croissant earlier. It had some fantastic looking cakes and tarts in there. On the basis of being one up, and trying to avoid rushing round big towns in the wet before everything closes, I might buy one or two to take home. I must be within two or three hours of Calais. Perhaps I could stop here – cheese and things.

But I need a box.

Did I tell you about 'my' box? The Poitiers box, when my wine was too heavy for the plastic bag handles? I was opposite a big pile of thrown-out cardboard boxes. I took one and it rescued the situation. Well, it got wet. I can't remember where now. I threw it away with some reluctance. It was a good size. I'd got fond of it.

Then, the Avignon campsite shop gave me another that I thought was too big. But I found a way of carrying it on the bike, and I grew fond of that as well. Well, in Trieste it got wet.

So, I'm boxless. Without a box my cheese-wine-cake transportation is a problem.

St Omer

Now I've got a chance to apply the Corkscrew Factor. I'll walk around Cambrai and shop! It's 11.15. Been here an hour and a quarter.

Excellent. I've just arrived at St Omer and parked in the central square. It's surrounded by tourist cafés and Union Jacks and English menus, or menus written in English. I thought I'd made a mistake. But I've walked down an alley and found a local bar. *Vin rosé*, I'm drinking. Cold, and enough 'red' to make it a good drink after a bike ride.

There's a big south-westerly gale blowing, and for much of the journey I've been blown about like a ship. Heading the wrong way at times and nearly losing control once – a sudden gust.

I'm home – at the Wagon, having a pint.

First I have to tell you about Phillipe and Dominic. We have to go back to the *vin rosé*. I decided on another. So I went up to the counter, or is it a bar? I said, "That was very good, *trés bon. Un autre, s'il vous plait.*" Well, Phillipe started to talk to me, and I stayed maybe an hour. Bought him some *vin rouge*, and he bought me *un grand café*. We talked about this and that in some kind of patois, and he 'introduced' me to the barman – Dominic. They gave me their particulars:

Baroux Philippe. Tongueuesse. St Omer.

Dominic – CAFÉ – L'EXCALIBUR – S'OMER.

At one point they were using an expression – rather, a sign – using the fingers and a kind of kissy whistle. This was used several times, so eventually I said, "What is this kissy whistle noise, and four fingers and a thumb grouped together, pointing upwards?"

This caused mirth and kind of brought the house down for about five minutes. Well, what it means is 'shitting yourself' when you're frightened. This explanation was accompanied by some fairly exuberant demonstrations. Bloody farcical. We were talking about going to England and Spain. Well, Philippe doesn't like flying – *par avion*. It was 'kissy whistle' plus four fingers and a thumb. Now what puzzles me is that they led me to believe that it doesn't happen to women, because they don't have 'kissy whistle' four fingers and a thumb.

Well, Philippe and I got talking about bikes, not then or after, but during the whole conversation. We had a conversation of about four or five topics going on at the same time, with Dominic trying to help with translation of certain words or ideas.

Can you imagine me not being in that bar, but staying in the square with all the 'tourists'? I was in France, pure and simple, only fifty yards from the 'tourist' area.

Eventually Philippe wanted to see my bike, so we walked back to the square. He helped me buy my croissants. Because the shop only had one, I topped up with four chocolate croissants. I hadn't realised that chocolate croissant is ideal with coffee. Why didn't I realise that? I'd not tried it. So, I've got the croissant but not the coffee.

I didn't tell you that I bought wine and cheese in Cambrai, did I? Well, I found this, as I found out, *cremerie* – kind of upmarket shop that sold fruit, cheese, wine, dairy goods, biscuits and things. So rather than rush round in Calais, I bought about £10 worth of cheese and a £5 bottle of wine – a red from the Loire.

Now I thought I would shop for more cheese in Bethune because I had space in my box. Oh, I bought two packets of coffee beans in Cambrai and the propriétaire gave me a box – sized between the Poitiers and the Avignon boxes.

Anyway, I set off to Bethune but when I thought I was there – because I was in a very nice town – I saw another *cremerie*. I now know that a *cremerie* is a better kind of shop. This man who ran it was marvellous. He gave me three cheeses and convinced me they were absolutely super. He wrote the names down. I bought a small tin of pâté, and left. It took me about ten minutes to pack this away. But when I rode off the man was at his window, waving me goodbye.

I love France.

As my father was Irish, I must have some Celtic blood in me. Is there an affiliation between the Celts and the French? Why do I feel at home here?

I've had a good trip.

I've just put my book away, but had to take it out again because I feel very emotional about it. It's more than it is??

I ought to have a section on the people I regard as 'relationships'. Not the new ones made, but the old ones who are part of my life. I would like to try that. It could be difficult for me to try and express something that, as Okri points out, is more complex than words can convey. But it will be worth the effort – for me.

RELATIONSHIPS

If certain people, my 'impassioned' friends – Trixie, Charlie, maybe R but she could be cynical – were to read my book, each would have different reactions. If Urline was to read it she might find it difficult to feel anything. Clive would, I believe, have objections to my interpretations of his course of action when Partheon is his main purpose not me. But Partheon – Clive and Sunny together – is more than a business to me. It's my 'emotional' but lost friend.

If I say that my story is less than adequate, which, in truth, it may well be, then I will be discourteous to those people I have met and found as friends: Claude, Laurence, Jean Luc, Bruer, Richard, Phillipe, and those I don't know the names of.

It matters that I do these people justice as well as those who know I am writing this journal – Rosie, Natalie. It matters to me too.

There's a fear about writing about relationships. Perhaps because much is not complimentary, or is only superficial. I say this before I have attempted it. I feel instinctively that this is the reason for the reluctance or the procrastination.

I have my immediate family – R, Trixie, Josephine and Charlie. Then I have my current friends; friends who are close but distant; friends who I wish were closer; and those I haven't seen for a long time – the friends you will always have, those that endure.

Josephine

I did a bit on Josephine earlier, but it was really more about me. Now, in her presence, I'm more impressed with my reaction. I understand at fourteen days there's no smiling or recognition, just 'getting across.' She seems to respond to my reactions. I've introduced her to Neil Diamond and Annie Lennox. I think she smiled.

I will have to refer her to Ben Okri as well.

What I think is nice is to see Trixie happy and content with her 'beeb'.

She's feeding her now, so I can't see Josephine's reaction to Annie Lennox. I'm not so sure that the reaction to a granddaughter is one of contentedness or happiness. I'm struggling to express something.

It's not that Annie Lennox or Neil Diamond are important: it's just the same with other human things – a sharing of something you find enjoyable or joyful. Perhaps it's Trixie and me being here, on our own with Josephine, in a nice house, a nice garden, plus some Alsace Pinot Noir – a good scene.

Should I feel something different? Perhaps I shouldn't worry too much about feelings, or analyse too much. I just want to be happy in a new situation. And I am.

I don't want to be compared to people who put on a show because that is parentally correct.

R wouldn't come over. That's disappointing. It's more disappointing because of her reason. She didn't want the kids to misunderstand our relationship!

R

R is my ex-wife. I visit her fairly frequently now. I do a bit of gardening and a few odd jobs around the house. She complains of not being able to cope with the size of the garden and the house as she grows older.

She wants to sell the house. I'm reluctant. It was my home. I have attachments. Whether these are the jobs I've done – two-way lights in the kitchen, for example – or the fact that I double-dug the garden, or that it is just nice to be there in the sunshine, I don't know. It's especially nice when the kids – Trixie and Charlie – come round. There's a temporary mending.

R and I have a relationship that I think I understand but can't explain.

I like being there. I like it that she understands me, even if she is wrong. I can behave normally. I think I get understanding when I have problems. We slip into the past form of behaviour quite often, but this stops when I come to leave to go home.

Routinely I kiss R goodbye. Sometimes she kisses me; sometimes she averts her head and avoids kissing. She says she doesn't like me to kiss her goodbye because I never used to. Now she finds it embarrassing. Always she waves me goodbye.

Well, people can change.

I like to kiss her goodbye. It's an affirmation that I might, or do, love her still, perhaps more than in the past. We may share some common problems as we get older. Her more than me as I have more cash, a different type of job, and get around more. I do what I please. R is more housebound, and uses the garden a lot for home-grown produce.

I feel that it is possible to get together again. We would need to sort out a few problems. R's not a problem solver. She accepts the status quo as immutable, and seems to accept that some aspects cause, and will forever cause, an adverse reaction. I think she avoids rather than resolves issues. She could be right if I accept that people don't change their characteristics easily. But I believe that we should attend to small irritations as an act of love, to enable us to become more loveable. To make it easier. To give the other person a chance when all of us have our foibles.

Do you get the impression that I love R? Do we know these things? This isn't the desire, the disconcerting desire man has for a woman in passionate relationships that we experience when we are drawn into 'affairs'.

I have been down this route. It is exciting. It is uncontrollable, though R would insist on the opposite. She believes that it is entirely sexually driven. I think it is more complex than that. To give up security for a relationship with such a fraught, perhaps futile, future, is irrational. That precludes a simple explanation such as sex.

There are common values at a certain level. In my case this may have been shallow, but this is the level at which much of life is conducted. Clean clothes, self-esteem, competencies, shared experiences, are very agreeable. Deeper attitudes – our interests and development – are temporarily put aside. These could surface in due course and cause problems. This could depend on tolerance and on amenability that enable people to adapt to another's values.

The odds of meeting such a person might be remote; thus we need to have adaptability and be capable of change. Perhaps only love motivates us sufficiently to change.

We have history now, of course, that might explain the reticence. I don't know what R thinks of me when I am least loveable. For my part, I don't like her 'knowingness' and her 'prescriptiveness'. It doesn't allow for discussion or disagreement. I got upset yesterday when R began to tell me what a poor personality my mother had, and how she had probably not given me as good an upbringing as I should have had. Well, all this might be true. But my mother operates within her competence, or up to it, and as far as I can make out, has never done anybody any harm in her life, wittingly or unwittingly.

Nor has Trixie told R that John's been married before. I suppose we are now in 'life's rich tapestry'.

R has a twin personality – or is this one of the many facets of the female personality? It's okay, I suppose, to have dual or treble personalities, but is one better or best?

My relationship with R has changed. I would like to cuddle her if she was equally inclined. To reach a common understanding is difficult for two people who have difficulty in expressing affection towards each other.

I still think that she is my wife.

Trixie

Trixie is difficult. Both close and distant. Since she was a baby she has been difficult to get emotionally close to. Pick her up to cuddle her and she would instinctively stiffen. From then on Trixie has always seemed antagonistic to emotional approaches. This is not just with me, because I have difficulties in showing my emotions anyway, but it's with R too, who is good at bonding.

I asked her recently if she liked being cuddled. You see, I can get close to people sometimes. She said that she does and it's with her boyfriends. Well I think I know what she means, and that makes her normal. But it somehow begs a few questions concerning her relationship with R and me. But I get close to her in conversation like this, which I think is more difficult for R.

The essence of this is that for some reason Trixie is unable to show her emotions to her mum and dad but I think she needs this more than anything else – she needs the reassurance. We somehow don't have the communication system – the means – for getting close. It's probably done by extrasensory perception, which is not satisfactory. All I know is that we have a bond of sorts – and Trixie is more sensitive to it than anyone. But she has a problem expressing it.

Her attitude, or her rebelliousness, has constrained her progress in the modern world. But in other circumstances she would have been humorous and perceptive. At the moment she seems constrained by her conformity with her peer group. This could be the fault of R and me. We positively oppose the diktat and conventions of society. This tends to exclude us, but we don't mind. But for Trixie this is anathema. She needs her friends to enable her personality to flourish. Whilst she carries a little of her parents' cynicism I think it might cause some embarrassment, but it leads chiefly to an arrogance, not perceived by me but by R. If I said any more it would get really complicated, and I don't really understand the situation now, never mind trying to add more innuendoes.

Charlie

Charlie is my son, and our relationship has been marred by my infidelity in 1987, when he was fifteen.

I don't recall him being fifteen, possibly because at the time he was small for his age. The previous summer we had spent three weeks touring France on the bike.

I was planning another trip, but not with him. I believed that he had spent enough time with his dad, and that he should develop other relationships within his peer group.

This period of our lives ended when the three of us – R, Charlie and I went to Leeds to look for a house and to start a new life after my 'affair'. It didn't work. I got out of the car at Harrogate and walked away. I took the train back to Cambridge.

I didn't see my son again for about three years. It was at the airport with R, and he wanted to know what I was doing there. He was going on a trip around the world. He was big, and independent. He had changed. I didn't recognise him. I still have difficulty. I missed this important period of growth and development.

By then he had gone to Liverpool University, having been on a trip round the world. These were vital stages and incidences in his life, of which I had no knowledge and played no part.

This gap is ever-present now. It makes me sad that I missed that period of his life and so had no appreciation of it, especially as R says that he needed his dad during this period.

Now, when we are together – we get on really well – I am conscious of the gap in our relationship. I wonder if he too is conscious of this.

We don't talk a lot. We never did. He seems introspective with me. But he's very outgoing with his friends. He's read Pirsig. And I think he likes to talk things over with me in a peculiarly detached way. I'll have to ask him one day to find out if he feels entirely at ease with me.

Return

I feel that to be nice to people is very productive in terms of human relationships. Bruer, also divorced, with his seventeen-year-old son Tjitte, made this point. I asked what it was that brought about our friendship. He said he could tell by the way I behaved or approached people. Whilst I probably have this personality I have learnt something on this trip – I think. I don't find friends like this in England.

I thought I had come to the end of my 'book,' but I think that what will be the end will be the meeting with Partheon. I will arrange this for next week, say, Wednesday. I'll ring tomorrow, then I can ask if they, or he – Clive – would like to discuss the French opportunity. I don't know whether to ask for Roland to be there. Roland now manufactures the toppers. I think he might have a better understanding of what was involved in my trip to two contacts. That would be 1500 to 2000 miles, I should think, on a single-purpose trip.

The other issue, of course, is my relationship as friends – would they be concerned towards my turmoil? Or will they find my need of them an encumbrance – an unnecessary and unwelcome encroachment on their time? Still, I'm nearly prepared for such an outcome, horrific though it seems in prospect.

I've come back to England and immediately find that I'm back in the same depressed condition about Partheon as when I left.

Rosie and I are meeting tomorrow. She didn't say she was looking forward to reading my 'book'. That's a bit of a disappointment. But that might not be the right interpretation of her attitude.

There are some friends I haven't mentioned in my book. I'm a bit guilty about that, but since it, or they, didn't come to mind, should that be a problem? Both Sally and Geoff have been good friends to me. I did think of sending Nick a card to let him and Geoff know that I was pissing off to Europe. But the writing and thoughts didn't coincide.

The other thing is, when I got back home I found a fax from 'Nick'. It took me a day to recall who Nick was. Perhaps I'm more of a friend to Nick than I realise.

It could be that my journal was an opportunity to 'unload' rather than list my friends and discuss them. I shall ring Sally today. She's important to me. So is Natalie, but I don't want to 'overdo' this. I rang her twice from abroad.

So, I'm all apprehensive about the future. I want to go back to France. Nick has offered me some work – market research into the sale of Nikwax products through primary schools, perhaps helping PTAs raise money for their schools.

When I took my cheeses to Cambridge yesterday R wouldn't come over to Trixie's, and Charlie was going to a party in Derby. I was disappointed Charlie didn't just stop in – he missed the Pinot Noir.

I left him some of the cheese – I cut all the cheeses in 'half'. I gave him the smallest half – is that mean? It's not an attractive part of my personality. I'm not generous enough.

I've just seen Rosie at the gym. We had wine – white, not rosé.

Rosie didn't look quite as enthusiastic about my 'book' as I thought she would or should. This is probably more to do with my interpretation. She said she wanted to read my book – and try the 'manuscript' version. I believe her. She is very supportive, especially about Partheon. Rosie's on my side. I don't know if I deserve it or not. I've told you I can put on this performance.

I wasn't performing this morning when I rang and spoke to Clive. I know I approached it badly but unless you express yourself, nobody knows where you stand. Now, it has offended Clive. This phrase of 'too much pressure' is not described. I said I wanted some empathy. He said he was too busy. Roland was pushing him for sales. I said we should resolve the problem; let's get together; it's not so much time as attitude. He doesn't want me any more, but he hasn't got the guts to say so.

I also spoke to Urline. We got on fine. She told me about Tom, her son, breaking his ankle. I told her to let him go on holiday, and expounded in part the Corkscrew Factor. When I said Clive didn't want to know as far as I was concerned, she said, "Rubbish."

I'm in this ridiculous position now of waiting for his phone call.

I want to bring the book to an end, not a happy-ever-after end. Partheon has played such an important part in my 'being' whilst on holiday – and before – that I feel that I need some sort of connection. This won't be a written statement. I think it'll be more a handshake type agreement.

EPILOGUE ONE

Pertinacity

I'd thought I'd finished writing, except for a report on my next or 'final' meeting with Clive Hope.

We've been in touch about France. It was a very difficult conversation. He nearly said, well he did say, "Well, that's it then," in the sense that that was the end of our relationship. But he held back from finishing his sentence. I don't place any great significance on that but it is important to me, if that makes sense.

I gave him a hard time – for him – I suppose. I raised the subject of my involvement, and he doesn't want to deal with it.

He's agreed to talk to Roland about the French development. Clive thinks Partheon should be there. So do I. Money will be a problem. Could I raise it for me? I would like the opportunity to try, I think. How about me in France, and don't involve Partheon?

Am I being an arsehole? I haven't told Clive anything of value yet, except that there's an agricultural show in September.

I've just seen Urline.

I'll tell you about that shortly, but first I need to tell you about Trixie. I ought to say that I'm in The Compass pub in Oakhill, waiting for Geoff. He's just arrived. But I need to continue this epilogue on relationships 'movement', no, 'evolution'. Is that better?

I've brought half a carafe of wine with two glasses, ready for Geoff. We had a good evening. He's been to France on a bike too. Then we went back to his place and I met his wife Kathy. I agreed to be the judge in their village play. What a chump I am, but in pursuit of a 'relationship' I do almost anything.

Trixie. I rang her especially to say I would like her to invite 'grandma' up to see her great- granddaughter. Trixie asked, "Why?" I didn't say so but perhaps I should have, "Because it's unkind not to." I sensed that Trixie is ashamed of her grandma, who's simple and now very forgetful. Well, we got into silences and 'seriousness', and I had to close the conversation in this state of 'tension'. So I feel that it isn't only the Hopes who are the only friends I haven't got: there's Trixie too.

When I saw Urline yesterday she said, "Hello, what can I do for you?" Well, anybody who uses that phrase cannot be a friend, can they? I find it obnoxious but I have to be nice – or try. It's this 'blackmail' business. They hold the power of friendship. This they withdraw, or have withdrawn. Any protestation I make about behaviour can result in me being finally cut out. I suppose if that is the position, then they don't care, and I might as well adjust to it and piss off out of it. Urline said she wasn't in a very good frame of mind because her boyfriend's ex-wife had died in a fire and was thought now to be a victim of murder.

I didn't feel for this situation. If I was Urline, would I be feeling kind of 'pleased' or 'relieved' that one of his former relationships was no longer available? This could be construed as totally insensitive and malicious. But in this journal I try to be totally open and I hope not to put myself in a position where I can be condemned for my feelings. Whilst I know people – possibly Urline – might read this, I can't afford to be discreet in my journal for fear of recriminations later. I believe most people have these feelings but don't bring them to the surface for fear of condemnation. Urline seems different. She may well have had a bad day because of this event. So I accept this. Whilst I got a very difficult reception and no indication of friendship, I hope it is just transitory. I've got this horrible feeling – is she self-centred to the extent that she considers the only effect she has on another person is adulatory? We like people, especially females, because we need that affinity of mind. Ian senses or knows this, but won't consider moving in with her permanently. If I was him, I would. I feel that whatever my relationship with her kids, I could work something out that would enable me to be with the woman I wanted to be with. That's rational, isn't it? Yet the reality is that he doesn't move in. Perhaps he is right to wait. It seems like he's happy to see her twice a week only. Is that mean and non-committal? Beyond that, I know insufficient about human relationship to pass judgement.

Since I believe Urline to be self-centred I don't think she's giving any thought to the effect she's had on me indirectly by influencing Clive negatively with regard to my future involvement in Partheon. Nonetheless, she did apologise for her attitude at the moment, and did pass on information regarding profit per month and the Partheon contact with de Lorgeril and

Gesret, so all is not lost.

I live in hope of a restoral of our relationship. I still don't understand what has gone wrong.

When I explained my position to Kay Harris, the psychiatric nurse, she volunteered the phrase 'let down'. She was referring to Clive but I think it's apt and also applies to Urline. Natalie is in a similar position. She has waited for Clive in the past, had to leave for 'baby', and the Hopes didn't contact her. It seems to me like a serious human failing in the Hopes.

I would like to see Partheon's financial performance. I could do my analysis and not bother them. I'll put that to Clive.

With regard to Trixie and my mother, I have to explain and describe the situation.

I live in a one-bedroom flat belonging to my mother.

My mother sleeps in the living room, on the settee. She's shorter than me so it's better that I have the bed and bedroom. It works but it's not the most satisfactory of situations. When I've got all the carpets replaced – I've had the double-glazing done – I'll look round for a decent bed settee and move into the living room so that my mother can have a bedroom properly. She doesn't care and might be afraid of me locking her away in the bedroom.

Anyway, because my mother is this simple soul, she doesn't impress anyone. So I think Trixie has this negative feeling. I do too, but I'm older and can come to terms with it. Sometimes I feel very emotional about my mother. She has her faults. I think she's an instinctive liar in order to keep up appearances. But on the whole, she's a 'good' person, has done no harm to anyone, and doesn't deserve to have lost her daughter-in-law, grandchildren or great-grandchild.

I feel like this. But Trixie must feel another way.

Now that there's some divergence between Trixie and me, I don't know how to handle it other than to be direct and to ring Trixie up and say I need to talk about it. But like Clive Hope, if this is a subject you would wish went away, you don't welcome anybody raising it.

Funny thing about my feelings for my mother. I moan constantly about her leaving food in the cat's dish. I think she forgets she's already fed him. So she feeds him again as she thinks he will stay away from home and stay with somebody else. She attempts to prevent this by keeping food in the cat's dish.

It drives me potty.

I'm sure that my 'bad luck' is due to my shouting and moaning at my mother.

The other thing is, I do some things for her, but when she's staggering about stiff, or with a bad leg, she sometimes leans on me and touches me. I don't like it. Why don't I like it?

I can accept she's forgetful – nearly – I'm more patient than anybody else. But sometimes I behave as though she's not got her normal faculties. For instance, she said, "Does it matter if I cut the old roses off?"

I said, "No."

Later, she said, "Does any goodness go back in the plant?"

I said, "No."

This went on for a bit so I said, "Go on then; cut them off."

Well, she cut all the roses off – buds and all. I was furious. She said, "I thought you said, 'Cut them off'."

Well, I can't see that I did, but I can see that for a forgetful person who hangs on to the odd word only, it might come across like that.

I think some of the 'bad' luck I'm having is recrimination for shouting at my mother.

Mrs Baldwin rang up yesterday. She's ninety. She told me her son-in-law, Bernie, who is sixty-six, drinks a lot and uses bad language. He lives with her in much the same way as I live with my mother. Mrs Baldwin is paralysed, and needs a wheelchair. She told me she was very unhappy with Bernie and she cried a couple of times over the phone. She thanked me for listening to her.

What shall I do? Talk to the Elderly Persons Service? I hesitate. They were supposed to call me last Wednesday but didn't. I think some of these bodies are useless.

I have other relationships: MacWilson, Preston's, Charles Orrel *et al*. But they aren't for this book. This book was for those that come to mind.

I have to finish this book now – I'm just waiting for the Clive Hope meeting.

It's like the end of the holiday. Chris called them the 'Going Home Blues'. I think I want to finish as soon as possible. I want to know what I've got. What I've produced. Perhaps, what do I do next?

It's Sunday, 13 July 1996. I feel very apprehensive. I'm afraid. Absolutely devastated. I feel that I ought to go to Partheon tomorrow morning, early. That means I should ring Clive now – after the Grand Prix. But it's the weekend. And I'm afraid.

How can I get rid of this upset? Clive has got control of my life. What I would like is to be friendly with all four; to be included in; to have sight of the figures, so that I can analyse them to my heart's content and to do something in France. I needn't take their time.

I'd like to do France. I will learn the language at long last and make a concentrated effort to find something to market in France.

I plan to meet Alex in Marseille in September, and this could fit with the show at Rennes.

Well, I rang Clive this morning but Sunny answered. Clive was with a customer. I asked Sunny if it would be OK if I visited Clive tomorrow morning. She said, "No. Clive has got a meeting with Roland."

Now that Roland is the owner of the factory that manufactures the toppers, and is a 50-per-cent shareholder in Partheon, I said that to meet him and Roland would be better. She said it wouldn't be a good idea. Now, does she know that exporting to France is quite a big decision? Perhaps they are just playing me for a sucker, and have no intention of selling in France.

I rang again. Sunny said Clive's not back. I can't ring again. She said that "France is work" and Clive will be tired. So I said I wanted to talk to a friend, but she just said, "Ring tomorrow." What a fucking cow. I feel hopeless now. I just want help from someone. I'm in a mess. I rang Urline, but she's busy. Urline is a possibility, but not today. Maybe when I have spoken to Clive. It's all finished, isn't it? I can't believe it's happened.

I want to escape again. Go to France. But I'm not sure it will be better. Who will take care of my mother? Can I afford it? Fuck it all.

I can't express what's wrong. I just perform. I write, I talk, laugh and joke. It's a mess.

I rang Natalie. She's good to me. Listens. Supportive. Must do something for her.

I have a lot to report. And I thought I had ended the book. But my 'perturbations' are in full flow. I have had an horrific euphoric week.

***

Big day today. The last day. It's all happened.

*I went to Partheon, prepared for most things but not for what
I got. I am going to tell you how I remember it. It'll be in
'chunks' – ill-remembered but surely not worse than by those
who also participated.*

*I knew at some stage I would have to say to Clive that my
information from the French trip took time and effort, and
I would be reluctant to give it to him freely.*

*But I knew that it would be mean to withhold it even though
they weren't going to pay for it. I would also withdraw
the 1992–1995 bill for my services should the situation
deteriorate. It's the theoretical charge of about £25,000 for
my contribution, plus the loan that Clive didn't want to see
about eighteen months ago, and didn't put into his Individual
Voluntary Arrangement (IVA). I accepted his explanation then
that in the IVA I would be sure of getting some money, but only
ten pence in the pound for my £4,000 loan. If the other bill
had been put in I would get little, whereas if it stayed out and
I trusted him, he would 'give me a lump'. When I said that this
means that I should trust him he said, "Yes, I hope that you
can" in the sense that I shouldn't need to ask.*

*I needed to leave Sunny with a statement of what I thought
she hadn't considered – what I thought was my financial
contribution. I also took a bottle of rosé for them in case
the situation, either good or bad, should demand it. I took
apprehension.*

*When Clive began to ask about the visit to France it was after
a period of hanging about. Sunny was busy. Didn't want to
spend time with me. Urline said hello, but it was obvious that
that was all she wanted to say. The body language was, "I've
no wish to talk to you." Clive began in friendly fashion to ask*

me about the trip, so I bit the bullet and raised my issue of reward. Sunny started on me at once – I think she said I offered to make the visits whilst I was on holiday: true. But I got the map of France out to explain where these places were, and where I had originally intended to go, and how this was a cost to me.

We also got into an immediate argument with Urline regarding the fact that she and Clive didn't support me with either phone numbers or addresses. I think Urline thought that because she had tried to find the phone numbers, she should be rewarded with some thanks from me. Well, she has a point, which under other circumstances would have pulled us together in a joint effort. But this didn't happen. I knew, and she didn't, that I was in France, without any idea where I had to go, and knowing too that no appointments had been made. I was a sucker. And now I was being accused of selfishness by wanting some form of recognition for my effort.

My apprehension was turning to sickness, so very early in the discussion I said to Clive that he might find me taciturn because I had put a lot of effort in and I wasn't getting any reward for it.

Bear in mind I can't remember what was said. I only give you an impression – my impression.

At this point Urline came in and I vented my feelings about the lack of support regarding no phone numbers, no brochures, no support.

So, this set the scene for a huge confrontation. Things got angry so I brought out the bill that Clive had never seen, for two and a half years' work with virtually no payment. I handed it to Sunny, who said, "Oh, I thought that was coming."

Well, clearly, we have a different situation now and I doubt if Clive will ever acknowledge that there is a bill outstanding.

Because customers rang up and Clive answered, I was ushered into Urline's office and subjected to being told what was wrong with me.

I said I couldn't understand what I'd done wrong, which they said was part of the problem. I was told that I wouldn't listen to Sunny's and Urline's criticism of my behaviour, so I sat down and said, "OK, I'll listen." I didn't understand what I had done wrong, but I would listen and try.

I can't recall Sunny's words, but they were to the effect of my persistence in ringing, my insistence to be involved and being around stopping the flow of work had a bad effect. This also upset Urline, though she couldn't explain it in words (I can accept this). I was like a rash that kept coming out. At one point they were going to ring the police to say that they had a stalker on their hands!

"Why don't you find somebody else. Go somewhere else. Leave Partheon alone. Pack up all your stuff to do with Partheon and throw it away," said Sunny, or rather shouted.

"What about the contribution I've made?" I asked.

"There you go again," they both said, Urline at the front, and Sunny behind me. "Every time you want us to tell you how good you are, how valuable you've been."

"I don't understand this," I persisted.

I can't remember what Urline said except that I wouldn't listen and that I was always mentioning what I had contributed to Partheon, and it got on everyone's nerves.

I expect it does, but to treat somebody like this is horrific. Urline was increasingly upset at me not understanding the nature and effect of my behaviour. My reply was that what was between us was personal, and shouldn't have been brought to work.

She replied that I was accusing her of some kind of vendetta against me. I said "Yes" or words to that effect. I had done the SMART application (a project management competition), and rang her up 'as pleased as Larry' that I had just made the deadline. From that time on it had all gone wrong. Sunny said that Partheon was too busy for my problems. I asked if my working through the night to meet the SMART deadline meant that I wasn't busy?

Sunny was shouting, and her dislike was very apparent. She said that they'd hoped that the French trip was a way of getting rid of me for a few weeks.

Not long after this Urline said, "I've had enough of this. I'm going home," and left.

At this point I knew that my time at Partheon had come to an end. I was both euphoric and indifferent. I suppose that I couldn't believe that it was real. I still don't. It's appalling. A tragedy. Nobody is in their right mind.

Because I'm not angry I can speak to Clive as though nothing had happened. When Sunny tells Clive to write the phone numbers down for De Lorgeril and Gesret, I object. I say they're mine. This prompts another outburst from Sunny. She doesn't realise that I put a lot of effort into this, and I get shit.

If you read my journal you can make your own judgement. Christ, it's cost pounds, and intellectual effort, to get that stuff. But if my intellect is of no great shakes, why didn't Partheon get the telephone numbers and find the locations and make their own contacts?

Then I photocopy everything – just like it was my office – give it to Clive, plus copies of Maslow's theory on Hierarchy and Needs, and page 4 of Ben Okri about friends and gestures. I also show him how to find places in France using the Michelin map and the postcode.

Clive then said to Sunny that she ought to calm down and treat the French question more calmly.

I wanted Clive to come outside to escape this attack, but he wouldn't. I offered a glass of wine. I brought out the bottle of Rosé. "Let's have a drink," I said. I meant it to have a reconciliatory effect at that point. Clive was game but Sunny said, "Some other time. We're busy." My bottle idea was good. It worked, but to the wrong purpose. It became duplicitous, not celebratory.

I wanted them all to write a sentence in my book. When all this started I had offered to shake hands with Sunny – a hand of friendship. She refused. So did Urline. She said she didn't know what to do. Clive accepted, and I told him he could rely on me and that I wouldn't let him down. I'll always be around.

Upon my having done all the photocopying, Sunny wanted the business cards I had brought. I told her that they were mine and she couldn't have them without paying. She told me to get out.

I left. Although I felt euphoric, I desperately wanted to see Natalie and Andy. Thank goodness they were in. We drank the bottle of rosé – Natalie, Andy and I. She gave me cheese and things. Good. Good.

I came home. It's about 8.30. I feel, or think, that I should telephone Urline. It can't make matters worse.

I ring her. "Hullo, it's Baroux." Long pause.

"Hullo," I think she said.

"I am sorry for any upset today," I say. "I didn't want it to happen."

Silence.

"Are you still there?" I ask.

"Yes," she says.

"Are you alright?" I ask.

"I can't answer that. I have to go out now," she says. "Thank you for ringing."

Urline has told me to consider that she is "a miserable old cow" and to get on with the rest of my life. Were it that simple!

Two days later I wanted to ring de Lorgeril in France, but I had left his card and telephone number at Partheon. I had photocopied everything for Clive, but unfortunately left the cards. Anyway, when I rang Clive for the cards he said he couldn't put up with anything like that any more. I agreed it was abnormal, but he then accused me of starting it.

He seemed to forget that Sunny had indicated that the French trip was a way of getting rid of me, and that I only wanted it recognised that some form of payment was warranted. That didn't have any affect. But it was clear that now Clive was no longer a friend. He refused to make any gesture of friendship

– his answer was for me to get on and do the French job and don't raise the matter of friendship or gestures again. Just do what was required. Visits weren't necessary but he would make some payment for my telephoning the contacts. .

I was appalled. After all this horrible behaviour he thought I could still work on behalf of Partheon for no money.

I'd never felt so low.

But next day I bit the bullet and rang for advice from Beryl, a mutual friend. I didn't expect to get it, but I did. I was not only given advice, I was given a little sympathy – just enough.

I felt cured. No more problems. I have, but not at the moment, and nor for the rest of the day.

I had arranged to see Natalie because I was so low, but Beryl had altered the low to high. Natalie must think I'm a charlatan – that I don't have a problem.

But I do have a problem, and I do need her to be around. I hope I can repay this. I'm going to buy her a present – some coffee and some tea. I've decided against alcohol.

Hellish times. But then I take my mother to Peppino's, the Italian restaurant, and the owner and staff make a fuss of her. And she gets a hug and a kiss from Peppino and she has had a happy time, and remembers it when she gets home.

I rang Clive this morning. Sunny answered. I asked if Clive would come out for a drink. She thought not. But I suppose I'll persist until I speak to him. The word is 'pertinacious' – stubbornly persistent.

It seems a bit like a dream or a nightmare – the contrast between the nice people around me and who I meet, and the Partheon trio.

I woke this morning – well, I hadn't slept really because the Italian espresso seemed to contain a lot of caffeine – thinking about Partheon and becoming totally depressed again.

But I've been typing my book – this book – and I've found the three letters I've had from Urline. I've just typed in the third. These letters are like islands of sanity in a mess of cloud-cuckoo-land. It's not insanity – it's something else. Let's call it emotional turmoil. And right at the moment I can see it more clearly. Urline was clearly having to contend with irrational behaviour on my part.

I could say I'm sorry, but that doesn't help. In fact, I'm the loser – I've lost a good friend. If you refer back to Stevenson's essay on 'Intercourse' you'll see that it is unlikely for my relationships to be restored. But, as nothing is certain in this world…

I might write to Urline to this effect. "Why?" you ask. "Why not leave it alone?"

Well, I like to try things out, give things a chance to go well. Remember the Corkscrew Factor? Not quite representative because I'm forcing it instead of opting for an alternative activity. But my personality won't allow me to give up when there is a course of action that 'ought' to be taken.

One of the problems I have is feeling in need of company, feeling a need to talk, and then when I do meet someone I switch unwittingly into 'meeting someone mode'.

Usually it begins, "How are you?" I reply, "OK" or "Fine." This doesn't dissipate the need to talk; it pushes it back into the recesses, brings forward 'the accept and the conversation' behaviour.

This means that the need to express is quashed. I don't know that it makes a difference. One 'answer' is to revert to writing, which I am now doing.

You see, I rang Clive, which took some courage in case one of the women answered. No one answered so I rang Roland. He took down a lot of details of my visit to Avignon. He will raise it at the meeting on Monday. There's a board meeting on Monday.

He told me that sales were below the level needed. So there's a financial crisis. Do I care? Of course not. I'm pleased. What a bastard thing to say. But if they want to do without me, then I hope that they don't succeed. Was I necessary? Unlikely, in the sense of not being indispensable, but could I have made a difference and still have kept my sanity and that of others?

Which half is it that's writing now? There's a half that can operate more or less normally, whatever that means, and a half that is detached from the body, and which is the half that feels everything. Is this related to Gestalt, *where the whole needs to be entire and not in parts?*

What does it feel? Is it me that is feeling? I believe it is me; it's just that I'm beginning to tap into my feelings. Perhaps not. These feelings are not happy ones, though I remember in France, particularly at Roc Suzadou, that there was a kind of contentedness at having experienced something good.

Right now I'm depressed because of Partheon.

They haven't made contact with me and I feel angry and frustrated. Both emotions are due to feeling that they are behaving badly towards me, and that I am unable to be nasty in return because that would bring me down to their level.

I'm sure that they feel justified in acting the way that they do, much in the same way that normal people can be persuaded to become torturers. Once you're in a culture that reinforces a negative attitude towards another group of individuals, then extreme forms of behaviour can be justified by the perpetrators.

I am missing my friends Clive and Urline. I am missing my involvement with the problems of making a small business work. And I am falling into an apathy, where I read no more, I listen no more, and I no longer associate with others.

I am becoming a zombie. I don't think this is depression. I think it is another form of mental abnormality.

It's all over, you see. No more Partheon. My epilogue will be the same as the prologue – a mirror image.

Will Day suggests I need a big steak and a good woman. Neither, in their different ways, has any appeal – the steak because I prefer alcohol, and the woman because she would be too demanding of my attention and loyalties.

I am possibly wrong about the woman, but I don't think that there is a woman around at the moment who would relish taking me on. But there is always the possibility. Isn't that what all the spinsters say?

Now, the reason for my writing wasn't just to express these feelings; it was to begin again the process of regular expression. To engage in a mental therapy and to use my pen again.

***

Return to Avignon

This was a five-day round trip to Avignon to see M. Chambert.

Two days there and two or three back, with one in Avignon – I can't remember. I didn't write on this journey; I just travelled. And since I'm writing in retrospect, I can't recall the detail. About 1,500 miles, mostly on the motorways. I think I got to Valence on the first day, and if I did, that was a huge mileage for me. That might include a stop at Troyes for coffee. I've no idea where I stopped coming back, except that I was perilously low on petrol on Monday in St Quentin. France closes on Mondays, but a young lad on a bike who I met at traffic lights guided me to a petrol station. So I had rosé and then ice cream to celebrate, brought some gungy cakes for my mother, and came home.

At Avignon I had, in the conventional English way, invited M. Chambert for a drink. He accepted and he led me to his home town – L'Isle sur la Sorgue. He then invited me to his home for lunch with his family. He has two little girls and his wife is called Virgin. We had peas and gravy followed by steak. Then we had a fruit *fromage frais*. This is when the lack of a common language matters – I couldn't convey my appreciation properly.

Then he showed me the model cars he and his brother were constructing. They were expensive replicas of classic cars for children. They were fully operational cars, with four-stroke engines, gearboxes, clutches, etc, and priced at about £8,000 each. I offered to sell them for him in England.

They were still at the design stage and were replicas of the French Delahaye of the 1920s' era. Beautiful cars.

Chambert's opinion of Partheon's toppers was that they were too dear relative to the Italian equipment he was already buying. We needed a demonstration. This would confirm that the SP – the self-powered machine – was good, and may verify that there is a possible market for this type of machine. When I reported to Roland the outcome of the visit, I think it supported his belief that the French won't do business with the English. I think it's more to do with failing to create a congenial relationship to enable the product to be given the chance to prove its worth. I would have liked to have tried it last year when there wasn't the hassle of personal issues spilling over.

La Grippe

I have come to a turning point in my life, I think. I don't have the compulsion to read management any more. It seems a lot of hokum at the moment, and it's perpetrated on the unsuspecting business community as a way of making improvements to an established system and to a firmly held set of attitudes.

I believe that a person's attitudes are based on their beliefs and values, which are difficult to change. There needs to be a passion for doing better and doing things well. And then we don't know if being good at something works commercially.

I think it is worthwhile for its own sake. The limits set by capability have to be explored if one's potential is to be achieved. There's a question that I would like the answer to: what is the mindset of people who seem to me not to strive for excellence, but merely what is sufficient? Perhaps it is just my perception, but I meet many people who seem to have answers rather than a spirit of enquiry.

I'm sure that Pirsig's notion of Quality preceding reason, is much the same concept.

To Françoise in Toulouse

Well, that's half the plan. I'm on the boat to Cherbourg for three purposes: firstly, to visit the 'La Space' agricultural show in Rennes to see what the market is like in France, and to conclude my relationship with M. Gesret. Without Marie Françoise we can't communicate. Secondly, to establish if M. Chambert wishes to do business. There are supposed to be prices sent and decisions made. Thirdly, to meet Françoise in Toulouse—Françoise is M. Lorgeril's secretary.

This carries with it another state of tension – R. This is a condition which has yet to materialise. It underlies every thought of another relationship. This is why Urline was so important – she didn't impinge on that state of connectedness with R. Françoise is a challenge in this sense – it's the 'see a woman in Toulouse' plan.

I have a reclining seat but I'm not using it. There's too strong a smell of feet. So I did my washing trick – face, hands, bum, feet. Oh, and under the arms. Must do them – isn't that the source of body odour?

I've also met Joy and Dave. They have a daughter, Daisy. Dave comes from Lancashire. Joy is beautiful and smiles and says "Wow" and "Super" and "Lovely", and lots of things like that. She's nice. So's Dave. Joy wants to know how I get on with Françoise. I promised to write. Well, I'm addicted, so it shouldn't be a problem.

I've had an English supper tonight – two bowls of chips and a bar of chocolate, two bottles of lager, and a couple of glasses of wine.

It's 1.30 a.m. We dock at about 6.00 a.m. and disembark at about 07.00 hours local time. I'm not tired and I have had no coffee. But as long as I get two or three hours' sleep I should be alright. I read that all right is two words. It is – it's recommended by Chambers, but it doesn't rule out 'alright', and since I prefer it, it stays.

Today's discovery of import is that my salopets are too tight in the leg for sleeping. I'd like to take them off but I've no trousers underneath and I can't get to the bike. (I'm still on the boat.) Rule 14: always put some shorts in the bag.

It took me all day to get ready – booking tickets, buying a new back tyre, riding an RF900 from Frontiers, topping up the oil, and generally panicking to try and leave in time for the boat. I left at 21.00 hours to arrive at 22.15 hours. Then as I was riding away from home it suddenly came to me that I didn't know my way to Portsmouth. I had to stop at the station and ask a taxi driver!

Coutances – with Cathedral

I've got several things out of the way. I have arranged to phone M. Chambert. I need to ring M. Gesret.

It's still a bit chilly for standing in telephone booths. Or is it just the effect of procrastination and anxiety. For some reason I am anxious, and not sure of my position about these phone calls. I wonder if this would be the case if I wasn't so uptight, or tense, about Partheon.

I'm coming, or have come, to the conclusion that Clive didn't want me involved in Partheon anyway. Sunny may have been behind this but Urline has actually done the work. Without Urline there was no contact. Anyway, enough. I have to attend to other things.

Souillac

Last night I camped in Le Lac Rouge – a farm. Nobody else was there and the owner's father brought me some wine that they make for themselves. It wasn't that good or wasn't to my taste.

They told me of a golf course nearby, which was run by an English company. I thought I'd call in to find out if they used toppers, and if there was an opportunity for Partheon. Jon Parris, the golf course director, who was English, said that the course was maintained also by an English company, and that the attention to the rough was not good enough. So there might be possibilities. He gave me the contact address in England.

Rennes–Bruz–Chartres de Bretagne and 'La Space Exposition'

I'm camped at Bourg des Comptes, where I met Jerome. He made me a salad because it was his trade – he worked in a food processing factory. In the evening I had parked opposite the local café and one of the locals, when he came out, came over and shook my hand. I don't know why or what he said. As I was in the 'Normandy Landings' area, perhaps he just liked the English.

Today I'm at Space '96. It is at the airport at Rennes, and is the main agricultural show for livestock in France. It's 13.30 hours and I'm surrounded by people eating. This is when the French eat, isn't it?

I would like to join them but I eat at night. Perhaps I should change when I'm in France. But a lot of people just eat sandwiches so I guess they will also eat tonight. The sandwiches look good, especially the hot sausage from Lyons. There's a big queue for them. The Lyons stand is pulling the crowds anyway. Looks like they eat sausages in Lyons. Perhaps I should have stopped there. I've only been to the *Office de Tourisme*. I've had a beer. So has everyone else.

I don't want too much beer. I'm meeting M. Gesret at 16.00 hours.

I arranged it through my interpreter, Carole. She came into a phone box with me so that I could communicate with him, and he is coming to the show to meet me. That's good, isn't it?

Partheon is bad. Just one embarrassment after another. No prices sent to Jerphanion, and I'm thinking that they are doing it deliberately to embarrass me. But Roland seems to think that Partheon had sent the prices. The trouble is that I have had to ring M. Chambert to ask, and it's been "No" now three times. What a ludicrous situation. How can he do business with a company like that?

I met M. Gesret and talked to him through Carole. He doesn't smile much and even though there is a language gap I sense there's no empathy between us. I told him about me and Partheon. That was a gross error of judgement. My selling trip is a lost cause. But I have met him, and in the immortal words of Jimmy Connors, "I am trying, for Christ's sake." He'll talk it over with his daughter and let us know. I've arranged that Roland should ring him tomorrow – Friday.

The women here are beautiful. Extraordinary.

Toulouse, Françoise and Failure

In fourteen minutes I am meeting Françoise in front of Frunch – a café in a hypermarket which I think belongs to Leclerc, and is located in a large shopping centre, *un centre commercial* (?) at Toulouse airport.

So here we are, taking coffee with Françoise – or am I jumping the gun? I couldn't find her office at the airport so I had to find a phone to contact her. One glass of rosé to give me the opportunity to write, and to prepare for Françoise.

The toilets here are good – large and clean. I could change from my motorcycle gear into civilian clothes so I would be more presentable.

Seven minutes to go. I'd better be early.

Françoise was late, but only a little, and she had only twenty minutes to spend. She should have been at work.

Françoise is nice – almost as I imagined her to be, though I couldn't have described her. She's my age – nearly – nice looking, dumpy and, I think, single. No ring but no chemistry.

She taught me to say 'cent' nasally – not 'song'. We talked for about ten minutes or so, and then she went back to work. Is that success or failure – coffee in Toulouse with Françoise?

Then I rang Roland to find out how he had got on with Marie-Françoise, and found that she had not been in. So I rang her and spoke to her. They do not want the toppers – they are too dear.

Christophe Chambert also says that they are too dear, so it looks as though my French mission has failed.

The only remaining chance now is for the golf course that I visited this morning to be the source of a favourable outcome. The golf course was next to my campsite, and as it was run by an Englishman, I called in. I gave them a Partheon topper brochure and spoke to the director – the Englishman. The golf course is owned by an English company, which also has an English company that is based in Essex to maintain its grass. So I have a new contact for Partheon. Clive will ignore it – it's from me, isn't it?

Roland told me that Partheon have an American enquiry which sounds good. This means that my efforts fade into insignificance.

Pity.

More than that – bloody disastrous.

But I don't feel quite so devastated when I write that. I now feel that the Hopes don't want to know me, and I have to come to terms with it.

I don't know what to do now. I feel very empty. I feel like Cinderella with the three ugly sisters. Perhaps something will turn up – you know, the Corkscrew Factor?

I feel angry about Sunny Hope, disappointed in Clive, and upset at losing Urline as a friend. I can't still believe that all three should be so totally cold and able to behave in such a damaging way.

Gaillac

It's time to eat. It's 8.30 p.m. in Gaillac and I've got an expensive bottle of wine – thirty-five francs. Local Gaillac. Plus sausage – *une piece*. Behaving like a tourist again!

Alban

But on Saturday I had the meal with Philippe, Yves and Marie-Jeanne at Alban. When I set off from Gaillac it was to get to Avignon but with a coffee stop on the way. Albi was too big, and I saw nothing appealing.

Alban was small with nothing exceptional. But I stopped at a café bar and asked for a coffee and a croissant. I was offered brioche at a table but I insisted on a croissant. One of the customers, Philippe, whose brioche it was at the table, then went over the road and bought me two croissants, for which he wanted no payment.

We got talking – and drinking – with him and his wife Marie-Jeanne and the proprietor Yves. This was about 12.00 noon. I left about 6.30 p.m., having been invited to lunch with all three at the proprietor's invitation. I did contribute a bottle of wine that I had bought in Gaillac.

Yves told me that Gaillac Blanc was the best wine – Perle Blanc Sec.

It was a remarkable experience. Philippe was an out-of-work lorry driver from Paris. Difficult to be sure as we could barely speak each other's language. This came in useful in a way because Marie-Jeanne tried to explain how to play cards, but I didn't want to play cards and I wanted to move on. Strange how friendships fit some occasions but do not extend into others. I think I was afraid of being invited to spend the night. Unfounded maybe, but the freedom and independence was the major priority. But I will go back. It was one of life's major occurrences.

When I left it was on Marie-Jeanne's suggestion that I camp at Nimes. But I didn't know that I was going to pass Roquefort. Nor did I know, though I know now, and I am unlikely to forget, that a dog had urinated on my helmet. I don't usually leave it by the bike!

Roquefort

Anyway, the smell got blown away eventually and I don't suppose it did me any harm, and I replaced it with another. I don't think I have eaten Roquefort. I have always thought it too dear. But I stopped and visited the caves and bought a piece. It's good cheese and I'm hooked. The story of Roquefort is probably part of the appeal, and I've been there.

I was supposed to put the cheese into the fridge within a couple of days, and to keep it cool. Well, it's destined to stay in the panniers in the heat until I get home.

After this stop I was still a long way from Nimes. So I decided to camp at Saint Affrique but only after some considerable indecision about either turning back or continuing when it's getting late.

Sebastien in Saint Affrique

It's Saturday night in Saint Affrique. I'm sitting drinking beer by a river by a bridge by a church, listening to music. It's coming from a typical French three-piece band with an accordion. People are dancing in the square in the centre of town. I'll have to go and inspect the situation. I can't make out how the accordionist is singing and smoking a cigarette at the same time.

It's the pianist. I would like to join in. But I don't.

I've met Sebastien. Sebastien is a chef in a restaurant in Saint Affrique. Odd, really – he's cooked in many countries in Europe, and he may go to Scotland next year. Sebastien drinks brown ale – Pelforth – with Crème de Cassis. Wow! Crème de Cassis is blackcurrant cordial at 15 per cent alcohol. Some French put it in their white wine. I could try that, but not with Pelforth.

He's written me a piece for my book:

> *It's midnight I arrive in my favorite bar near the restaurant. I meet a man an English man 'Russell'. I speak with you Russell you are alone in a little country St Affrique stay to speak with you and it's good, good to meet some people. So now I write my adress*
>
> *Sebastien Viev*
>
> *227 Avenue dr docteur cultien*
>
> *12400 St Affrique*
>
> *I hope Russel you find more than a job becouse you're a man who try to find something and I'm sure after your travel your find what you want so be happy be lucky*
>
> *God Bless you Russel*
>
> *Sebastien Viev*
>
> *Pays des Cathares*

I want to write to someone. But I've found that when I write to several people I write similar things in a different way. And I don't have a record of what I have said. When I write a journal or diary I don't worry about differences – there are none – and I don't worry about what I have written because I have kept it.

I could write the journal and send photocopies to my friends. Would they feel cheated? It would be too impersonal. I can't copy what Sebastien has written three or four times. Well, I could, but it wouldn't mean as much, would it?

Avignon for the Third Time

My writing is bad because I've drunk about half a bottle of wine and one beer, and it's only *dix-sept heures et demi*. I've just bought another bottle of wine from the campsite shop – a special promotion – so why not try it?

I'm getting the days wrong. Today is Monday. I've just returned to the Avignon campsite having visited M. Chambert at Jerphanion. I invited him for a drink, and we went to the village where he lives – L'Isle sur la Sorgue. We only had one glass of wine. Then he invited me to his home to see the car that he is building. It's a small replica of a vintage French car. It's meant for children of eight to thirteen years old and who are the children of the rich. Christophe Chambert is making the body. His brother is building the mechanics. It is priced at about £8,000 and he said there's a market already. I offered to sell them in the UK. He is interested.

So there's a tenuous connection still with Avignon.

I don't know that there will be any further business with toppers. Chambert thinks they're too dear by about twice – double. I suggested to Roland that three for the price of two would be a possibility if Chambert wants to try them and find out more about the market. The trouble is that we cannot demonstrate them here to prove their worth.

Yesterday was Sunday, and I travelled from Saint Affrique to Nimes in order to camp. But even though it was late, I decided that I preferred to limit the number of pitching and taking-down sessions of the tent, and press on to Avignon.

On the way to Nimes I called into a farm – a *domaine* – to buy a bottle of wine. A kind of shambles but, my god, the wine was good – eighteen francs, Cépage Merlot from Pays D'Oc, Domaine Des Olivier, J. P. Bezzina, Moules and Bancels, 34190 Ganges. I would like some more but I'm not returning that way.

That decision to call at the farm was made after I had gone past it. This is significant because my mentor when I first joined NAAS (National Agricultural Advisory Service) (Food) was Harry Wright. He was an ex-Fleet Air Arm pilot, good at his job as an adviser, and very precise. I liked Harry. His philosophy was 'Never turn back'. I have tended to adopt this ever since, but on my trips to France this year I *have* turned back. I've inclined to use judgement or intuition – not a rule – and to be more decisive. I think it's worked well. After all, it was by turning back at St Affrique that I met Sebastien.

As I've had dinner already I'm not sure how to handle my evening meal. I've got the wine. Perhaps some bread and cheese. I've got some sausage left that I bought in Gaillac. That was good. So was my Gaillac wine, but at thirty-five francs it should be. I found that I had had enough after only half a bottle. So that was interesting. And if Gaillac Blanc is better, then it's really good. Des Olivier was not as good but it was better – translate that into French if you can. I mean that Olivier's was nearly fizzy and had a peppery effect – very moreish on this occasion.

The half-bottle I drank went down in about five minutes. I didn't mean to do that, but it was there.

Well, it's nearly 5.30 p.m. I'll go to town and find a photocopying machine, buy some bread and cheese, and then I may have a beer.

I've had the odd thought in the last few days that I'm 'on borrowed time'. Does that mean I'll have to pay for or pay back the 'time' I'm spending on these French trips?

I've failed in a business sense, though I did call into the golf course at Souillac. Partheon have a fresh contact out of this. But if it's 'my' contact Partheon might reject it on the 'not invented here' syndrome. I'll ring the contact when I get back, to find out what has happened.

Villeneuve

This is my second visit to Villeneuve, and this time I've discovered towers and walls and forts. Villeneuve was important in the tenth century for defending various *abbés* and kings. I've become a tourist this evening, and it was quite interesting. People live in the old buildings and within the walls. I should have spent more time here.

There are four women and five men drinking at two cafés in the square. They are all extraordinarily good looking, except one. He keeps me company.

I wonder what would happen if I went up to that lady with the red hair and kissed her goodbye – or hello, come to that. It's a three-kiss routine here. In fact, it's not routine. One man has kissed her – well, she kisses; he presents his cheek! And he's still there.

I was going to mention Sebastien before I came out this evening, but I didn't stop. I had the feeling – it's much less now – the feeling that I was living in another world. What Sebastien wrote seems quite extraordinary after being in his company for only twenty minutes. It's quite different to what I've been used to. And the only thought was that whilst it is of interest to me, just what interest does it have for others? He's talking about me. For you to be interested, should he be talking about you?

I've spent too much on food: Ten francs on custard flan, twenty-five francs on *museau à la Lyonnaise*, plus some cheese. And I plan to have some chips and beer when I get back to the campsite. Perhaps tonight's purchases will do for tomorrow as well.

I'd better go – they close at 8.30 p.m.

I'm heading north and it's raining for the first time this trip. Guess what? My replacement oversuit is not waterproof. Are they going to believe me back home? I want to know who these bikers are who don't complain about this.

This morning I'm in Orange, aiming to buy some *verveine* soap and some Provençal serviettes. In a nearby café I had coffee and *pain de raisin*, and saw another customer writing with a notebook and pen. I thought I could strike up a conversation, though I was writing at the time. But the attempt failed. When I approached I asked him in English what he was writing. He said, "A book", and that was that as far as he was concerned.

"A novel?"

"No. A book," he replied.

"Is it fiction?"

I think he agreed with that and added that he was a writer, but I couldn't make any more progress.

I've got to press on. It's nearly four o'clock and it's cold in these mountains. With wet bum and some wet clothes from Avignon, I need to be lower down and a bit warmer

The next town is Le Puy and after that, Clermont Ferrand. Perhaps it's too optimistic to think that I'll make Clermont Ferrand tonight. I've only got about two hours of biking time left.

And I can't answer the question of why I need to get home so quickly. I'm getting close to the decision to stop when the moment occurs.

I've done a hundred miles today, so that should be enough in a way. That is a six-day trip rather than three. I think it is a question of opportunity. I do not want to hang around or to wander about on the bike. I want to make progress, even if it is only to get back home. After all, I do have my VAT to do. Christ! Can you believe that the real world is VAT? I don't want to know.

What do I do? Write to Sebastien and Philippe and Françoise?

What about Partheon? Are they a dead duck for me? Shall I send them my message? "Cinderella is alive and well and knocking about France." Is that too nasty? I think it is apt though. I've met some nice people and they think I'm alright. I've told you that before but I'm reluctant to give up on them. I've read somewhere – oh, yes – in the *Harvard Business Review*, that Confucius said that there should be reciprocity: "Do unto others that which you would like done unto you."

I think my Cinderella joke is funny, that's all. They might not forgive me. After all, they probably think I deserve what I get and that they are behaving properly. But to reject somebody can never be good, can it? Let's go.

Le Puy

I stayed in Le Puy last night and met Bob. He was a Canadian, forty-five years old, hitch-hiking around Europe. I met him at the Youth Hostel. It was closed and we were both hanging around outside, wondering what to do next. He asked me where I was from, and we exchanged information about where to stay instead. Apparently, there had been an accident in the hostel, so it had been closed prematurely.

I was directed to a campsite, and Bob to a hotel. He told me that he was searching for work to supplement the cost of his trip, but this had been thwarted by the French restriction on the employment of foreigners. So instead of using buses and trains, he was hitch-hiking. He had been to Poland, Czechoslovakia, Hungary, Germany, and now France. He had an ex-wife too. He had been a salesman but now was a tiler – laying floor tiles.

I'd said that it was likely that the Youth Hostel would be about the same price as the campsite and I should use them more often. I think that this might have indicated that I was trying to economise and because he, too, is short of money he suggested that we share a room in a hotel to share the cost, and it would probably be cheaper still.

I rejected the idea and said that I preferred to be on my own, and I feel very mean about it. It might be that it is a missed opportunity for another relationship. I'm not matching the friendship I have been offered by the people I have met on this trip.

I think that the reason for my refusal was the prospect of getting too close to another person and so losing my freedom of action – independent action. I not sure I understand this. It's a trade-off, isn't it? The loss of freedom is a gain in companionship. The risk is that the gain does not sufficiently offset the losses. It's a rare event for gains to offset losses, but when it happens it is huge and mutual, or so one hopes. And with Bob I decided against the risk.

As we continued to talk I suppose I tried to compensate for the rejection by offering him a glass of wine. This is where my glasses paid off. We finished off my bottle in a back street in a medieval part of Le Puy. I suppose it was a memorable moment for both of us, but marred by my decision.

In the morning, having 'struck' the tent – I've just remembered what the opposite of 'pitching' is – I went into the old part of town and had a cup of coffee a hundred yards from the cathedral. Just like Avignon. Coffee close to cathedrals is lousy. Is it a mistaken marketing strategy? The supplier has a captive and transient market and so doesn't have to bother about quality.

I have deviated from the Clermont Ferrand route and cut across the Central Massif to Bort Les Orgues. This is in the heart of the Massif. It isn't as I remembered it from my trip here with Charlie in '86. It's green and wooded, not scrub and heat and sparse and isolated communities. I'll find it next time.

I've not made much progress in these last two days. A hundred and thirty miles yesterday, a hundred and twenty today so far. It's 4.15 now, so there's time for a few more miles. I hope to eat in daylight today. Night-time eating is not good. It limits the exploration of the town or village. That's not good because the judgement made of the town, such as Le Puy, is made on limited information, and probably flawed.

I prefer the smaller towns. St Affrique was good. I didn't tell you that I went to a disco there. I saw searchlights and went off to find them. I ended up in an ex-monastery, I think it was, that had been converted to a disco. The guy on the door let me in to show me around. There was no one around, and I left for the dancing in the square. Towns like Le Puy are too big for that kind of discovery.

Peyrat au Chateau

I made progress but because the sun was shining, or nearly, I decided to camp around six o'clock. At this time the next site on from this village was closed. But a little further on was a house with a field, and it was a site owned by an English couple. I had doubts about stopping because of 'the English', but thought it might be a new experience. It was another instance of 'turning back'.

In many ways it was a new experience. The owners were in England and the house was being looked after by an Australian couple, Maurice and Barbara Chapman. They were on a six-month trip to Europe and had met Afreda and Chris, the owners, somewhere, and just fell lucky. I've suggested to Barbara that if the owners want a houseminder in future, then call on me!

No one was in when I arrived so I pitched, showered and then sheltered from the rain. It then rained for more or less twelve hours, and it's not looking too good today.

Maurice and Barbara invited me to eat in the house with them. I took my food with me. It was an old farmhouse with a huge open fireplace. Some of it had not been repaired but most was as you might imagine an old French farmhouse to be. Idyllic.

They were farmers, and grew sugar cane on two hundred hectares. Barbara had a degree in sociology and in business. So we could discuss Maslow's hierarchy of needs!

Because sugar cane no longer paid, they had started to grow vegetables on a five-year rotation. This made some money, which together with a few windfall inheritances plus Barbara's budgetary control skills, enabled them to tour Europe – Turkey to Norway.

I'm cold and have some wet washing, so I'm reluctant to leave. So here I am in Peyrat. Maurice asked if I would like coffee this morning, or would it spoil my espresso? I said it would, so he told me about the two towns nearby where I could get my coffee and come back and talk.

I tried Bouganeuf first. It was further north and further away and larger than Peyrat. But I didn't like it much so I've come back to Peyrat. I've had two coffees here. They weren't very good but I had them with croissant and *pain du chocolat.*

I prefer sitting in cafés to viewing cathedrals and castles. I'm happy to see them at a distance. The architecture and the environment is very pleasing. I like the way the French have, and live in, medieval towns, but the café life is more interesting.

In this café the woman behind the bar, the proprietress, has just offered her cigarettes around to all of the customers. I've asked why, and she said it was just as a present. Earlier a customer came in and went round the café shaking everyone's hand.

I've got a big dose of inertia here. It's 12.30 and I'm not making any effort to move on.

I got back to the house about 2.00 p.m. and talked with Maurice. He talks a great deal – do I? – and it was about 2.45 before I got round to the decision to leave. The washing was still wet but the inclination to leave was quite strong. That didn't last very long. It started to rain so I took the washing in and started to pack. But as the rain got harder I decided that taking the tent down would risk getting it wet inside. So I packed everything, left the tent and abandoned the plan to leave. Now I'm back in the bar in Peyrat, reading Proust and drinking coffee and rosé. It's time I started *Contre Saint Beuve and other essays.*

I bought some Pinot Noir at the wine shop earlier, but instead of drinking it here I've decided to take it home. She didn't have another Pinot Noir, so I have had to settle for something else for tonight.

It's been raining heavily for about two hours now, and the locals are just strolling about in pullovers. They then come into the café expecting, I suppose, to dry out without too much of a problem.

I left my bike in the square next to a tourist information stand. It is covered, so I've put my panniers under cover in the dry with my gloves and overgloves. My wine and beer are in the panniers. I hope that they are still there when I get back.

Maurice and Barbara have invited me to tea this evening, so I've bought three cakes. I'll buy another bottle of wine and perhaps some more meat. I do have plenty but I may need a variety for appearance's sake.

Barbara is also writing a diary. I wonder if it is anything like mine. I still think that mine is insufficiently interpretative, but I think this is a matter of time. Perhaps description precedes interpretation in order to have a topic. There may be another way of doing it. Proust is using a word that I don't know the meaning of – *pastiche*. It is in neither of my small dictionaries – English or English–French.

There could be one in the house.

This rain is ridiculous. The girl in the tourist office not only forecast this but said it will continue until Monday. It's Thursday today. I need a plan – like 'Go to Youth Hostel'. Is it time for this?

Mid-Channel

I believe it's Saturday, and I've made it to the ferry. It arrives in Portsmouth at 9.15 in the morning. Is that Sunday?

In many respects I've done well these last couple of days. Last night I made it to Alençon and stayed at a Youth Hostel for forty francs.

I also had a meal out. Very expensive for me – 180 francs. I had beer, *pierrades* and crêpes. The wine was Saumur Champigny. It was all excellent. *Pierrades* is raw meat and salad – I had duck – and you are given a hot stone on which to cook your meat. In addition there was *gratin dauphinois* – is that right? – with three different mayonnaise sauces.

The crêpes were apple in a pancake bag, cooked in or with a liquor or spirit – *flambé*. The liquor is lit and then poured over the pancake. I could have done with a good shot of cream on it but that might have spoiled it.

It's just occurred to me that I called into Poitiers and revisited Café de Gambetta. I thought of calling in to see Lauren at Motostart, but again I felt it would be a bit false. What I did do though, was to go to the *patisserie* next door and buy some flan. It looked so good and at Fr6.50 it was cheap. And it was big! And it was super. Guess when I ate it. When I came back from my fancy French meal in Alençon. I was just going to have a taste! But it was sweet and cool and creamy and vanillary and had sugar crumbs on top!!

I ought to stick to coffee; it's less fattening. It would be too easy to have a French holiday going from *patisserie* to *patisserie*. I've advanced from croissants. I'm going for the black belt in gateaux.

Today was cold and murky at the start but when I arrived at Fleurs the sun was shining. There were a market, traffic jams and crowds of people. I had just parked the bike when I was persuaded to support the handicapped and to part with thirty francs for a packet *brioche*. Was that my good turn?

I was amply rewarded by ending up in a café that I was directed to, and where I had two excellent coffees. In addition I had a couple of French pastries from a *boulangerie* round the corner.

The coffee, I discovered later from the menu, was *rouge* – 25 per cent robusta and 75 per cent arabica.

On the menu there were three other coffees: Colombian, Mocha and Costa Rican – pure arabica at twice the price. I tried the Colombian. I'm reluctant to tell you but I preferred *café rouge*. Does this mean that the secret to good coffee is to get the robusta content right? How do I buy robusta?

Then I went back to the *patisserie* to buy some cakes to take home. I thought it was a bit premature but I'm generating the policy of trying to be always 'one up'. It works, I think. I stopped at a supermarket to buy a corkscrew, decided against it, but then found myself in Cherbourg too late to do any last-minute shopping or have a meal. I'm not badly off. I have got three bottles of wine from Saumur, I've got the Roquefort—ill-kept but I have faith – and I've got a bit of Vacherin: a small piece of cheese for thirty francs. Boy.

Because I was too late for a meal I brought my wine, cheese, bread and pâté up to the saloon. I also bought a bowl of chips and some Guinness, and dined in unusually ordered style. I also gave in to *pain de raisin* and a Twix bar. I somehow regret having a can of Guinness and a half-bottle of wine. I enjoyed it at the time but it was greedy.

I would like to report on my feelings but I'm feeling the effects of overeating and overdrinking – a motley mixture, and I'm not keen on sailing or travelling like this. It's a five-hour trip – the same as the air flight from Cyprus to London.

Good Advice

The French, despite their adherence to culture and cuisine, are a mite short on paper in the bogs. Knowing this to be the case leads to the situation of crossing the main square with a pink roll under your arm, advertising your intent, whilst all the world's beautiful people are observing you over the top of their *sirop et café*. Although I have expressed a preference for the squat toilet, it does not lessen the embarrassed feeling of the forthcoming undignified posture and the careful arranging of motorcycle leathers and, on occasion, oversuit. I have found *une aide par excellence* in the form of a pack of twelve packets of ten *mouchoirs trés doux*. These are handkerchiefs made from cellulose, and stronger than toilet paper. The essential essence of them is that a single pack can be carried in any pocket and you can tear them into smaller pieces, I found, if things get a bit prolonged. You can hold your head up high then when you get back to the bike, and pose in comfort and contentment.

I've had the feeling today that I may have come to terms with the Partheon situation. I'm still very affected by their treatment of me. This trip has perhaps triggered the thought that I might have had greater compensation than Partheon could offer. How can I have counted for much with them if they can dispose of me so easily and so viciously?

I feel like making, well, in fact, in my mind, do make, nasty remarks to Clive, Sunny and Urline. But I feel that this is not good and will not help any more. I'm concerned about Proust's remark regarding enmity and former friends. I shall endeavour to avoid that.

When the sun shines in France I consider my other friends. How can I be other than well-endowed? This ignores the friendships I have experienced in France. I bet Partheon hasn't met Yves or Philippe or Marie-Jeanne. Nor Sebastian. Nor stayed in a French *gîte* with an Australian couple, drinking wine and coffee and eating French *patisseries* beside a log fire. Then slept in a tent in the pouring rain.

Epilogue Two

The three letters I received from Urline are islands of sanity in a mess of irrational behaviour on my part. I've lost a good friend. Impossible to restore, difficult to replace. When I made one last effort she said, "I don't like the way you are talking to me; I don't want to talk to you again. Thank you very much," then put the phone down.

Shit and derision. This is kicking the body to make sure it's dead.

I spoke to Clive later, crying down the phone to him.

"Nobody at Partheon can cope with your behaviour. You should get yourself sorted out," he said.

"OK," I said, "I'll do that. I'm seeing a psychiatric nurse; it's all going to happen." I'll call on Tuesday to see if he'll come out for a drink.

Meantime, I call Françoise, de Lorgeril's secretary, to maintain and advance my contacts and relationships. You see, I'm pertinacious – stubbornly persistent – and I kept ringing Françoise despite feeling that De Lorgeril might have lost interest.

She gives me another name to contact, which was progress. Whilst talking to her I propose that she takes me for coffee in Toulouse when I'm next in France. "Any time," she said.

So, I do have chaos theory and the Corkscrew Factor working on my behalf!

I've got a date! Manic.

Avec Françoise, il y a t'espoir. C'est tout?

I've had more communication with France, and established a relationship with M. Chambert, my new contact. He's in Avignon, and gives me enough information for me to believe that there is a market in France for a specific type of topper.

When I convey this information to Clive, Partheon have a meeting. But they decide not to proceed with the French opportunity. They can't afford it, they say. I also think my involvement had influenced the decision. Sunny is not going to let me get a toehold again. I think this because when Clive told me of the decision he also said no to a drink. The two women are putting a lot of pressure on him to have nothing more to do with me. We agreed not to communicate any more; it was creating too much unpleasantness for him.

I try to talk to Clive yet again, but Sunny is very short with me so I talk to Roland. He says that Partheon owe him £130,000, which suggests that they are in trouble. I hint at bypassing Partheon and selling straight from Roland. He's not in favour of that but agrees to put the proposition to Clive today, Tuesday, the drink day. Sunny takes my call but it ends with her putting the phone down. She doesn't want me anywhere near Partheon, and that means France is out. But I do speak to Clive and he says yes to a drink and yes to France, but needs to talk to Roland first and will call back. For the hundredth time he doesn't call back, so I have to ring him. He's still in the meeting so I say to Urline that if Partheon don't want me to ring, then Clive has to tell me. They thought he had, and that I was going to sort myself out. "No," I say. "Clive was going to have a drink with me." She seemed surprised.

"Trying wrongly to do right," I hear Stevenson saying.

When I convey the decision to M. Chambert he said it is ridiculous. So I ask M. Chambert to speak directly with Clive Hope. M. Chambert tells me that Clive had asked him not to deal with me, but I think M. Chambert has some empathy for me and agrees that we meet when I'm next in Avignon.

And that is going to be soon.

I'm so bloody annoyed at all these blocks I try to buy two machines from Partheon, via Roland, to take to France to make sure that M. Chambert sees them in operation. The mind works overtime. I think it's such a good machine that I don't think it would take much to convince somebody to establish a plant in France. There's a possibility that Clive is aware of this and is trying to keep me dangling with Partheon.

I dismiss this as a thought too far for Partheon, and I've given my word to Clive that he can rely on me. So I break my agreement about communicating with him as it seems stupid to have this development without direct and regular communication. Aren't we better to do things together, when doing things alone would be less effective?

Clive agrees. So we are going to communicate illicitly. And my buying machines is unnecessary because Clive believes M. Chambert himself is going to buy and arrange shipment. I'll check this out. Pertinacity!

In the space of forty-eight hours we moved from arguing to co-operating. Roland is inclined to go along with this but is aware of the female factor. Of course, Clive has got to keep to his side of this arrangement but I can always contact Chambert to keep things moving and up front. Hence the haste to get to France.

Well, that's not quite right. I also have to meet Françoise.

The importance of this is that it carries the promise of a common interest and shared pleasures. This is the essence of the difference between friends and a companion. I have friends who have been, and are, extraordinarily good to me. But I do not have a companion. And this is where George Eliot and Urline came into my life. And left.

I still feel bad. It comes and goes. I've been trying to settle down to some French 'homework' but it eludes me. I just pace about. These pills are no good. I need to talk to Partheon *et al*. Still, a couple of shots of rosé makes things better – and writing my journal. It would be interesting to discover if being accepted by Partheon again would put things right. Perhaps it's unreasonable to expect people to have a 'change of heart'. The fact that the phrase exists suggests that it can happen, but it hasn't been my experience.

When Clive rings he says no to France and no to a drink. The two women are putting a lot of pressure on him to have nothing more to do with me. When I suggest that I should stop ringing him he agrees. I lent him £4,000 and worked a lot for nothing for about two and a half years, on an increasingly involved basis – first, as a kind of consultant, then as a kind of contract worker.

I'm devastated. Not so much by the lack of reward, but by the end coming in such a way.

I think I'm still a very good friend of Clive's. Perhaps more so bearing in mind that the end was so gentle and non-judgemental as regards him and me.

But the women, whose attitude appears to be to protect Clive by being vicious to me, might, in their quieter moments perhaps, reflect on their behaviour and regret its effects if not its outcome. Yet people – that is me – cannot warrant such acrimony. Perhaps they will lie on their deathbeds and feel that their actions were justified.

Perhaps I will never cross their minds again.

I don't feel anything, really. It is unreal. I have no comprehension of what has brought this about. Being intense with Urline was a precursor, but not immutable, and nothing that couldn't have been rectified in a congenial way. Christina used the word 'flipped'. And her training was in psychology, so maybe intensity does trigger a violent backlash in order to break the relationship.

I've had four friends ring me tonight, one offering a room for the night when he gets his new house. If I said the hurt arising from the loss of Urline and Partheon is greater than the value I place on my four friends, would that be understood? I don't want it to be taken as a statement of values on a two-dimensional measure, but more of the presence of a thorn that's small and sharp and gets to the core in places where the emotions wax and wane and puff out.

Dear Partheon. Didn't I do more right than wrong? Don't die. Don't grow big. Just be my friend.

When I started this journal I posed the question of whether it should be a continuum from my 'outpourings'. I think I concluded that they weren't separate, and therefore I would continue. The same question applies to the present. Is it part of the future, or should I stop writing 'the journal' and, if I need to write, then begin something else?

What's happened is that I've had 'multi-occurrences' and I haven't recorded them. I'm not with my book.

Yesterday – an age ago – I rang M. Chambert to tell him that Partheon were not interested in business abroad.

Right now, I feel light-headed. Quiet. Paused.

I've just rung Clive and we put things right. Have we?

Just before I rang Clive I had spoken to Sunny. She put the phone down on me again. She affirmed that Partheon were not dealing in France, they had no money, that I was no longer welcome at Partheon, and that Partheon would not want to sell me two toppers or have me represent Partheon. I was trying to point out that I had relationships to deal with in France, that her attitude was unreasonable, and that there was some unfinished business to do. That brought a negative response. "Leave us alone – alright?" she said.

"What about the money you owe me?" I asked. That was nasty. But she's got to attend to it, in my opinion, by making some kind of statement of intent – either to pay or not to pay.

But the phone went down.

I rang Clive on his mobile. This is dogged persistence. 'Feel the fear and do it anyway' has been superseded by 'Carry on until the job is done'. 'Feel the fear...' is a valuable means to that end but could be misinterpreted as a bloody nuisance, but much of what I'm doing involves others who are not party to this maliciousness.

I told Clive that what we were doing was bloody silly. He agreed. So we arranged to work together on the French deal and let matters blow themselves out. He also told me that Urline was going to ring me because she was concerned. I felt magically better.

Now I've made arrangements to see M. Chambert.

In my mind I was going to try and be useful to him in his dealings with Partheon. I have a lot of information. I could perhaps get a job and make sure that the machines were of good quality and in sufficient numbers to meet the market. And if my relationship with Partheon was finished, then we could either buy or make.

That was a resigned aggravated feeling.

If I'm better, and don't need the pills, what are my friends going to say? That I've fucked them about something awful? Perhaps I can pretend again – that I'm ill.

Diana

Right now I have an idea, interrupted by having to start the computer.

It is to do with death and Diana. I'm affected by the death of Diana despite my thinking that somehow she was giving a performance to counter her privileges. Then my mother seems to be suffering from a pain in the chest. "Could this be her demise?" I ask. So the thought of death past and death to come brings about the emotional response which I do not fully understand.

I can rationalise and expound on my biased view of Di and the car accident, but this is merely a description. My mother is a good person and not in any way a lesser person than Diana, yet there is something different. Di was privileged, beautiful and had elements of hardness in her make-up, characterised by her TV remonstration against Charles. Yet she found it necessary to devote much of her emotional energy to causes that we in society have wrought yet reject, whereas society worldwide has lost its compassion, and has become more obviously mean and selfish. Diana had charisma, which, as I understand it, is the public display of those aspects of endeavour, rectitude and compassion that we, the ordinary people, aspire to but are not capable of portraying. In Diana's wake, we realise that we needed someone with that high profile to bring such perspectives to the world's attention. She had the propensity and resolution to display publicly her own values, which is what doubtless made her different. She, like us all, made her own values, and manifestly, she chose non-competitive, non-economic issues. I fear, however, that hypocrisy rules and fine emotions do not influence behaviour sufficiently. Adam Smith's 'invisible hand' was wrong. The law of the jungle lacks certain human values – concern for others, which is not a sufficiently powerful marketing or egoistic ploy. My mother's concern for others was impressive but restricted. She did not have the charisma of Diana.

My own contribution was not to dig up a beautiful geranium to pot and lay outside Buck House – I thought it would be a 'performance' on my part. Perhaps it was a lost opportunity to make a point. Instead, it's still in the garden and is, in my mind, Di's geranium.

I joined the Prince's Trust

Crete

"If a man does not keep pace with his companions, perhaps it is because he hears a different drummer. Let him step to the music which he hears, however far away." Henry David Thoreau

Florence

Anna gave me this paper. I knew I would begin this piece with two names. This morning I went for a walk around the bay to the side opposite the 'Practice Place'. I had no compulsion to walk, but I did. I discovered that I had no will to stay still. A bit disturbing because at the Practice Place I should be calmer. I am calmer, but it's difficult to be still to read, or just to sit.

Now I'm writing, and it's a great pleasure. There is a great urgency and passion to let it out and put it down. And on my walk I knew I wanted to write, but had no paper. I knew I would begin with Florence. And if Anna gave me some paper, then that is how I would start.

I need to tell you about both Florence and Anna.

You see, I'm in Crete, on my yoga holiday. It's October 1997. My first trip since last year's trip to France. I'm disregarding my trip to Dijon in March. That was to a seminar and it is different.

Right now I'm at a table in the shade. The sun is just moving across the page, making it too bright for writing, but there's no point in me moving. We begin Thai massage in a moment so the participants are gathering round with Brian the teacher, and his girlfriend, Yoke. Brian is a beautiful guy. He moves in a slow, graceful, measured way, and he has a nice gentle manner.

I met Anna and Florence on the first day. Anna sat down at the table I was at and Florence, her roommate, joined her. Soon others came too, and we discovered that Florence was French and worked in England. That was last Saturday, the day of arrival.

Since then we have eaten, mixed and done our yoga practice and generally got to know one another. But from time to time Florence and I have talked together and found that we have a common interest in philosophy, and she has offered to help me with my French.

Florence and Anna are young. This makes it difficult to form a relationship. It is virtually impossible for me to make suggestions for spending some time together. Yet Florence behaves in a way which leads me to believe that she is comfortable with my joining them – Anna and Florence – on the beach.

I have been several times, which brings me to the present, almost. Yesterday, Anna decided to walk back from the taverna early to have her massage with Fiona. Florence and I, or Florence, agreed with Anna's suggestion that we might take the long route back: a path through the olive groves.

So Florence and I walked back together, first in the evening sunlight and then in the moonlight. We did not know the way, so we took the wrong path from time to time.

In the evening I did not join her at dinner. I would have liked to have done but I considered that she needed company other than mine.

Hence my walk round the bay this morning. And this morning Anna gave me the paper. Florence has noticed that I am writing. After Thai massage

I had a brief word with Florence, but now she has gone somewhere else.

This is all a bit descriptive, isn't it? Too oriented to boy-girl romance. It is either not like that, or it is more than that.

Everything about Florence is French: her looks – but what does that mean? – she is certainly attractive; her hair is long and plaited, and either hangs down or is wrapped round her head; her walk, a bit side-footed; her dress; and her interest in philosophy, stemming perhaps from her school education. It would be nice to have a little contact after we leave here.

At the Practice Place much of the discussion is about yoga and its effect on a person's life. It tends to be metaphysical – if I understand the word – and the need to be both selfish as well as selfless: to do what we want to do, otherwise we won't be good at helping other people.

I can imagine R being quite cynical at this. At my 'getting involved with young women' again. But I like Florence's company. And I like Anna's company. And I like the company of other guests too who are also women. But Anna and Florence are special.

I am extraordinarily lucky to experience this, even if it stops now. I am only using my senses so far as to what is acceptable to others. As a last resort I could be bold, take a risk, and say what I think and feel.

Urline has already informed me, or taught me, not to misinterpret signals from women. I don't think I do but I bear it in mind now. It might be that I take in the implications with some precision but my reaction is too intensely dependent on the friendship.

So, other than write, I must find some other activity for my free time. This is after the massage, which finishes at 2.30, and before yoga at 6.00. Right now I have no wish to swim or socialise, even though we have some new guests.

Alan has just asked me if I had a good time at the weekend. I told him about my walk with Florence and that it wasn't a good time, but that it was something better than that. I need another word, or words.

Florence and me in the olive groves.

Anna

Anna's not here. I need to write about my relationship with Anna.

Anna is about the most beautiful girl you could see. Dark. Beyond description. Young. Talks in metaphysical terms. Has been to many places in the world.

It was Anna who linked me to Florence. But now Florence doesn't want to communicate. The emotional high has crossed into emotional sadness. Still worth having. A brief encounter.

Today is Sunday. I need to include Anna. She is important. She has been very nice to me. Anna is one of the world's nice people.

Tonight, I kind of rejected her at her table. There wasn't a proper place, so I thought, so I sat at the next table with Florence.

This is when I confirmed that Florence is now indifferent. I think that Anna has been consistent. I was like Clive – lacking integrity and switching allegiances. Perhaps allegiance is worth talking about later. This is to be about Anna.

She's delicate and vulnerable though very strong. Believes in spiritual things and has a totally different behavioural pattern to me. That is, she meditates; looks at people in a different way. And only by my having more discussion with her will I be able to explain this.

But isn't it worth being here? When I've told you about Florence and Anna I can tell you about the men here.

About Dave; I share a room with Dave.

But it's not time for Dave. He's rock solid. It will wait. Anna and Florence are ephemeral. You have to catch the moment.

With philosophy I believe that you need to be very clever – in an intellectual sense. Sartre talks of the self (my word) being isolated (my word) from other selves. When we need to interact – in a human or sociable way, the self, endeavouring to form an object in the world, will compete with other selves doing the same thing. The result is a form of conflict.

This is my current interpretation of my, not the, current circumstances.

I am emotionally affected. I'm not calm. It's due to my interactions with Florence and Anna. Had I met no one I would be writing much the same, except that I can recall with much pleasure my experiences. Here. At the Practice Place. Perhaps that raises the Practice Place to too high a level. It's other people with characteristics, formed I know not how, possibly with like experiences, who emit not contention, but 'attraction'.

I need to think about that – it's not attraction. It's something deeper than that.

Why do we suffer dashed hopes? I can't see the purpose. A better provision might be a guaranteed warmth. Perhaps insecurity draws us together to limit disappointment or its effects, and reserve or contention is needed to protect against inertia. But sometimes a rock-solid arm on the shoulder might be essential for one's well being.

Tonight, it was easy to do that to Sasha. Yet, it may not have been welcomed. It depends on whose arm it is. Sasha has a problem with alcohol. I was walking the dog from the taverna when I met him this afternoon. I had been forewarned of Sasha but I didn't know who he was. But I met him. He bought me a drink and he admitted to having a problem, but he could crack it if he had to. I think we made some sort of contact.

At one point I assumed my counselling role and asked him, "What would it be like if things were better?"

Without too much thought he replied, "If things were better, life wouldn't be worth living."

Tonight, whilst I was upset about Florence and Anna I could, and wanted to, put my hand on his shoulder and say Hullo. I did but said "Goodnight". I was behind him but I think he knew it was me. Florence was there. I hope I was not putting on a performance.

I must stop now – my writing is not letting it out. It's cramming it in. I feel too emotional to continue. I will, for a line or two, because obviously I can, but not to the point of pulling out the essential emotional point or feeling. It's this inability that causes me to stop.

Camel

Camel is the dog. He belongs to the taverna. Camel is tied to a tree all day and it was Yoke who, when she was walking Camel, met us on the way to the beach and implied that Camel needed guests of the Practice Place to take him for a walk. I had no intention of taking Camel for a walk but when I went out, completely at a loss as to what to do, I passed Camel and also saw Florence, who waved. A few minutes later it occurred to me that I could go and fetch Camel and see Florence at the same time.

And I did. And that's how I came to meet Sasha. Well, I had this lousy evening cavorting about in a sports vest, showing off my physique, when I decided to cut it short, after saying goodnight to Sasha, and go to bed. Sleep did not come. I've been hooked again on this emotional embrace – Florence. She is 'formidable'. But you know that. I've backed off to give her 'space'.

The trouble is, that it doesn't work for me. What a stupid counsellor's pat phrase! 'Doesn't work' means that Florence's space restricts mine. I've nowhere to go.

During the night I got up and went for a walk, and met Camel again. I do not know whether he recognised me or not. I talk quietly to him and he tilts his head. I don't think he quite understands it. After such a fitful night I didn't think that I was in any great shape. Yet I have done two yoga sessions, Tai Chi, Thai massage, and had a massage from Fiona. I also walked Camel for a short time. He wasn't keen on my taking him up the hill so the walk was short. But I feel OK.

Well I would, wouldn't I? I have partnered Florence at the Thai massage – at her instigation – and we literally got to grips with one another. I have also shared some other moments with her and Anna and Alison. So I'm happy. I didn't talk to her about 'feelings' so I've avoided the 'intense' bit, and I'm 'better'. Well, not quite, but the happy part is larger than the despairing part.

I do not know if Florence is beautiful or attractive or not. Certainly not like Anna. Maybe a hundred times more. But it's not mathematical. I've told you what I like about her – her face, her hair, her walk, her dress, her way of talking, her interests, her strength, her grace, her vulnerability. I don't mean that to be emotional claptrap, but strong, attractive people are at least as vulnerable as the less strong and attractive. The less strong probably have fewer sycophants.

I would like to have Florence and Anna as friends, each for different reasons. But there is thirty years between us. Perhaps I'm lucky. I don't get involved in 'relationships' which I can't cope with. R might, and probably does, regard me as somebody led by "his dick" and who should keep his distance from younger women. I wish it worked like that! But I regret that she isn't able to share in what I regard as 'good' experiences. Perhaps she does but I think not. R is ultimately my security.

Florence is my being, and Anna too.

In a society where being angry plays no part, it's a peculiar feeling of not knowing what to do now that I've 'fucked things up'. Even the word is inappropriate.

Today has been eventful. First, Anna is ill. She virtually collapsed this morning before Astanga yoga. She has been complaining of a stiff neck and pain in the shoulder. She walked into me in a kind of daze. She had to sit down. I would have laid her down but she was surrounded by others who wanted to help – Anne giving Shiatso though her feet, Alan massaging her neck, others offering glasses of water. Arkadi, the Russian masseur here, then gave her a massage. She appeared to recover a little but has been in bed since.

I thought I was to have a massage from Arkadi at four today. He's not here. Perhaps it was three! That's what I mean by fucking things up.

Also, I'm giving my writing to Anna for her to read. There's so many people around her that I can't really get near. So because my writing is a bit related to Anna and Florence and because of my 'condition', I'm letting her read it. I wasn't sure about letting her have the 'emotional claptrap' whilst she is ill but I have an opportunity and decided to take the risk. She's nearly got it – Kathy will give it to her. But it might be that Anna doesn't improve and has to go to hospital, in which case my 'writing' will end up in the garbage can. Rubbish or not – I would like it back.

Before my massage appointment I took Camel for a walk, for about half an hour. I don't think that he enjoyed it. Whether that was because we went along the beach or whether it was because of me, I don't know.

Anyway, no 'deep' or 'painful' massage from Arkadi to compare with the softer touch of Fiona. *C'est la vie*!

I'm stuck now. With no massage, I've missed joining a group. I'm on my own and I don't like it. I thought writing would be good, but it's not. I don't want to dwell on my failing relationships. It may be a good time for a swim but this is a poor substitute for a displacement activity. Life becomes increasingly lonely.

Yet I ought to remember that today is Trixie's birthday. My daughter is twenty-nine today.

Alison and Kathy

Tonight my spirits were up. Florence was going to give me some French practice during dinner. I sat at an empty table just before the girls came to the terrace where the dining area is situated. Kathy, Alison, Florence and Anna came and joined me, which was a bit of luck. Kathy sat opposite me, which on another occasion would have been a great delight. We talked about rationality and logic compared with intuition and chaos. Kathy argued that all was rational, all could be explained. I found it difficult to argue against this despite believing the opposite. I hoped she was wrong. Kathy is a former body-builder, and has entered into competition. She knows about muscles and diet. I think she is in the middle of a difficult relationship at home, which is manifesting itself as a form of illness. I think she has read about a dozen books since she has been here. Inasmuch as I should judge, she is extraordinarily intelligent. She has a firm view on matters psychological and is very quick in her responses. She has a sort of cynicism about men and would like to have one, but keep him in a cupboard until he's needed. I think the cupboard is there. It's just that she is in it too.

Anna was next to me and Florence was at the end of the table, talking to Anna and Alison, so I didn't get any French practice. Anna left early because she was feeling poorly, so once I returned from getting my second course I sat slightly nearer to Florence. I started to say things in French, which cut out the rationality discussion. I was very discourteous to Kathy. Quite soon she left.

When Florence went for a cup of tea I started to talk to Alison about Scotland, how I spent three days of my honeymoon in the Borders, and had had a major row with R. This started a discussion about relationships because I said divorce was not a break, but a longer leash.

No one can forget or eliminate their past. It affects all future relationships. I don't want to hurt, or risk hurting, R a second time. I don't know for sure that I would, but I am unwilling to assume that our relationship is completely broken. I don't think that is the case. Therefore a new relationship, even if the people are undamaged, is easy, especially when they carry uncomfortable appendages. Alison considered that this was all in my mind and so could be dealt with by modifying it. I did not understand how emotions and beliefs could be modified. It was yet another interesting discussion harmed by my partial attention to Florence. She joined in at one stage, but soon got up and left.

This caused another great welling of upset. I couldn't continue the discussion with Alison, which was unfair to her. Alan at that point came over to ask if he could join us and also to tell me that Dave would like our room free for a while.

Alison told Alan that we were talking about relationships, which he would enjoy – it is his professional subject. He is a consultant, dealing with stress and related issues within companies. But I felt unable to cope with infecting others with my issues so I asked them to forgive me, and went for a walk.

When I came back I was at a total loss so I took a risky decision – I went to Florence's room, where Anna was in bed talking to Alison and Florence, and Kathy was on the balcony talking to Alan, who I joined. I was somewhat out of sight, sat on the floor and said nothing, and nothing was said to me. Then Dave arrived and started talking to Anna, so I knew our room was free.

A little later Alan and Dave went off to the taverna. I should have gone too but instead I thought I'd go back to my room and drink a little of Dave's vodka. But as I left, Florence came out especially to talk to me and to say that the reason she left the table earlier was her feeling unwell, and not to do with me.

Transformed. Happy. The roller-coaster has gone high.

Monday

> *You have left my life*
> *Before having entered it*
> *So much loss*
> *Too little time*

Yoga

We've had eight days of tuition and practice: Astanga yoga – the continuous movement form; Iyengar – the precise-posture form; Thai massage, which uses light pressure on the body's meridians together with stretching; and Tai Chi – the slow martial art. Two yoga sessions in one day is unusual, but I find it quite easy. Most are dropping out and, of the original group, only Alison and I are left.

As a result, I think my posture has changed a lot and I am getting more muscular. This might be due to weight loss since I cut out the brunch. Breakfast and lunch are served simultaneously at 11.30, and are too much. I was beginning to swell around the middle. Fruit and yoghurt is sufficient until dinner at 8.30, hence the weight loss maybe. Others put their lunch in a box to eat later. So, apart from the niggling injuries I came with, I'm in good physical shape – plus a tan.

This is the type of holiday where the mental state will be affected too. I have no desire to have a 'good time' and I'm happy just to be here. Had

I not met Florence and Anna I might have spent more time with Alison, possibly Fiona. I could spend more time with Dave and Alan but I think the males here, and that includes me, want to meet the females. The men see each other enough, probably, at meal times and in the evening if we are in the taverna at the same time. My feeling right now is that I can't have the company I want so I don't want any. And that is no good to anybody. But when you see a person on their own, you do not know if the person would like your company or not, or even you theirs.

I feel it is necessary to record my mental state because I do not find it easy or even possible to recall it later. I was having a coffee with Florence, Anna, Alison and Kathy in the local taverna, and it was extremely pleasurable – I feel that is a stronger feeling than 'pleasant.' It was especially good because both Alison and Kathy were there. It is also easier to be in Florence's company when others are there. Florence has told me that she will talk to me about my 'letter' to her and Anna later. I had a great need to ask the question of how one captures the 'pleasurable' moment, to retain it. I wanted to write the question but thought that would be an intrusion, and spoil it. Although Merleau-Ponty proposes that the language of others can change the way we see the world, it might also, for the individual, help establish the feeling through expression. I did ask the question of the group, whose response was 'to be' and to 'experience it'. But I would also like to know what I would have written.

Yoga is as much about people as about the physical activity. There's a greater faith in spiritual matters, less interest in the material aspects of life, and perhaps less on the rational. It has been a revelation for me.

Arkadi, the Russian guy who does massage, has just said he will be with me in a moment. Pleasure multiplied.

I wonder what Florence will say. I saw Anna alone on the beach yesterday. Semi-planned. I thought she was with Florence. I didn't approach immediately – I swam and did another 'stand-off'. But when I went up to her she was meditating. I waited for a while, then went off and came back later. A strange, comforting experience. Boy, am I lucky. We talked for quite a long time. She said that I should talk to Florence.

I am writing in the dining area. Gingi is giving Alison some extra tuition in Tai Chi. Gingi is an amazing person. Just nice and cheerful in ordinary circumstances, but in Tai Chi he becomes inscrutable, blending expression and clothes together into perfect movement.

I still want to know about pleasure. If we have corticals or cortices that respond to stimuli it suggests that there is no mechanism to retain it. The person needs the stimuli to be repeated. So what do we remember? Is it the same as remembering where I put the car keys? That seems inadequate for the more intensely pleasurable moments. It must be more than that – sufficient to draw us back but insufficient to keep us in a constant 'pleasure' state. Perhaps I don't want to remember them in that way. I want to absorb them. For them to be part of my being. To recognise or reflect on or retain the intensity. To avoid 'happinesses' becoming losses.

One of the things I have chosen to do is to write. I enjoy this. I mentioned this in the conversation. This seemed risky because I worried that it might not be favourably received. It was OK at the time but walking away to write was maybe dramatic. I was quite highly charged, and feel a bit foolish now. Well, not really – just me trying to make contact.

"Dave, read my fucking book."

What is happening? Jesus! I have been to the taverna with Florence, Anna and Dave, and got into a big argument about belief in mysticism – alternative beliefs. Dave seemed angry with my scepticism about Rheiki. What's Rheiki? Tonight I cannot explain, but it's a form of 'metaphysical' energy that has healing properties and can be transferred from one person to another.

Unfortunately Dave, who is my roommate, took my stance as a closed mind. I don't think I have a closed mind, or agree with his suggestion that my questioning of a belief positively prevented my benefiting from it. The background to the argument, which was ignored, was that Florence had spent a couple of hours with Dave in our room finding out about Rheiki, in which Dave professes to have skills. I wanted to know why he hadn't offered it to me! I figured it was a gender issue, not a mind issue! But the focus of the argument was on my closed mind, and I got angry. A belief in mysticism means to me to lack faith in other views and statements.

Dave wanted to know what I thought about when I was riding around France. I felt that an open answer at this point was appropriate and said running out of fuel, the sensation arising from the poplar trees and the landscape, and of being in France. Dave was surprised and said that he would be thinking of the people he would be meeting.

I lost my composure at this point and shouted, "Read my fucking book."

The girls started an alternative argument, trying to break Dave and me up. Anyway, we held hands and tried to experience the flow of energy round the group.

I don't want to be like this. I'm not sure what this is. I would like...

I don't want to cry like this.

It's fucking stupid. What am I?

The girls said nice things. And Dave too. Is this experience going to affect or influence my beliefs?

Fuck! It's about midnight. I'm on the balcony outside my room in Agios Pavlos in Crete. Does it matter where it is? The sky is virtually cloudless. It's warm enough. There are stars. Earlier was a full moon minus one day, so it's pretty light.

Why do I behave this way? What does it achieve? For Christ's sake, it's not just a performance, is it?

Florence and Anna must think they could do without it.

Friday. Last day. A time for mourning, or sadness? Well, that's the theory. In Italy, last year, it was 'Going Home Blues' – a need to get home. Here it's different. Here, there is a group of people who know one another in varying degrees. A kind of sadness – leaving a friendly crowd – but not the same. The emotional experience of Florence, Anna and Dave has been too great. I'm in a constant state of apprehension, one reason being that it's been a lost opportunity for making friends – a possible last opportunity. Friendships don't come easily any more. There's too much judgement. Something that drives me to solitude – unwittingly.

When these occasions occur – and Urline and Florence are two such occasions – I behave in a way which destroys them. Not that either had long-term potential – no potential beyond the circumstances that cause it to happen. But what sort of relationship is it that doesn't have an emotional response, a period of closeness beyond the normal, when experiences can be shared, when words are no longer necessary? When, as Okri says, smiles and warm gestures are important.

I thought that I'd managed this at first. In trying not to impose my company on them my detachment caused me to go intense – a self-imposed rejection. The balance was wrong – no warm gestures but an awareness of their lack.

To try and influence a relationship seemed wrong. Others seemed comfortable: Mark was always with Sandra; Dave went round and spoke to everyone.

Right now, Florence is twenty-five yards away, on the balcony to her room, Cathy is ten yards away, at a table at the taverna, Alison is at a table at another taverna, eighty yards away. All three have walked in a way which suggests that they want their own company. I may look like I want my own company, but I would welcome any to join me. I don't think it would be appropriate for me to join them. I believe we know instinctively how to behave such that it doesn't cause discomfort. Of course, nobody else might be feeling lonely like I am. All three women have a viewpoint on 'life', 'projection', and 'assertiveness' – a way of behaving which prevents those things happening that they don't like, or doing something about it if things do happen. None of these things will be wrong, but too much control-behaviour precludes my kind of intense response to emotional circumstances.

What might be appropriate for me is what I am doing now but in public. Revelation to the group about feelings. It need only be brief. An early-morning warm gesture can be given or received to make the rest of the day go better than it otherwise might. Perhaps it is idealistic to think that people might help others or want to be helped by others, in a society where strength is a valued characteristic.

I value strength in myself and in others but I still feel that groups are better and that group strength is greater than the sum of its parts. There's a group on the beach made up of the people who work at the Practice Place. They appear to be very comfortable and happy. Sufficient contact to keep each other well.

That is only surmise. I am only speaking of my needs being met. I'm not sure about my meeting other people's needs – R, Trixie, Charlie, Rosie, Alan, Victor.

Friendships are awkward. We are selected by other people, or we select them. But there is a distance that we need to keep, particularly as we get older. The element we refer to as 'space' has as major constituents the factors of time and solitude. Time for ourselves, to be on our own but with our friends still available to us. But there is more to it than this. Friends are not like wives. Friends are demanding of our attention and this is wearing, but wives are not – we can be together yet in our own small world, albeit shared. In addition, friends have their characteristics which we seem to endure for the benefit of the accord that we share. I wonder if this is what Sartre is saying but in code: "I know perfectly well that I don't want to do anything – to do something is to create existence, and there's enough existence as there is."

I wonder if my sitting here is causing people to avoid walking past, and I am thereby blocking the path of people who would otherwise walk past Alison. I'll walk a bit and make myself scarce.

Alfa Class F

This is the day after the race. But that merely identifies it. For me, a considerable amount of living that has taken place in the last twenty-four hours.

Charlie was racing his Sud in the Alfa Romeo Owner's Club Class F race. To get that car on the grid was a major achievement. What is in that lad that I didn't know about? He had a couple of friends helping him, plus the advice of one or two other drivers that he knew. Julie, his girlfriend, was there. And I was there with Florence and her friend Sarah.

He started last and came last but he had a great race with Barbara, who was in a '33'. He said that his engine wouldn't rev above 5,000 but he did manage to overtake once. This was at Craner Curve, the part of the circuit from where we were watching. Barbara had more power with the '33' – a very competitive car that belonged to her husband, so she soon regained her position on the straight. Nevertheless, first race, an overtake, and overtaken – better than just cruising round somewhere in the middle with no one in contention.

I didn't stay with Charlie and his race crowd afterwards. Florence and Sarah had arranged to go to the pictures, and they invited me along.

I chose to go with Florence and Sarah. What do you think? It was no clear-cut decision. I sensed a conflict of interests within me. I could have stayed with Charlie and been part of the crowd. Or, if things were normal, on the outside. But to be with Florence – and Sarah – was a friendship that was totally impossible to reject, whatever interests it cut across. It was as if my life was being replayed in moments, with an added dimension of experience. I knew there would be certain losses, my gains possibly ephemeral, but, as the Mary Chapin Carpenter says, "I pay my dollar and I place my bet; I take my chances every chance I get." And Charlie? What did he think? Pleased for his dad? Embarrassed by his dad?

There is no right answer to the quandary. My life is important to me and if I can be happy, or try, is that not best for both me and Charlie?

Dad is acting with propriety, in yet another dimension, with his 'chances', with his past, living his life.

There comes a point when you might feel that life is not worth living and, in depressed state, end it. But, sometimes, the opposite can be the case. A life so full that it seems that that is the time too. An emotional cul-de-sac, where all the feelings and emotions are crammed and cramped into a small space.

It's not just Charlie. I went back to Birmingham with Florence and Sarah, and Florence invited me to stay the night. There was some farm accommodation fairly near, so I'd already decided that I wasn't going home in the cold after the cinema.

That evening we discussed our personalities and our relationships a little. Florence attributes her outer shield, which she describes as an armour, to her father. He is extremely clever and capable, and her obligation, as the eldest of the three children, was to match her father and be successful.

I slept on the sofa, well lay there, because in the flat above my kind of music was being played. I enjoyed it, just drifting in and out of sleep. I thought of going to join them. It was just as well that I didn't. I had imagined a 'like Florence' couple. Instead, it was a group of three or four young people already in Florence's bad books for playing music too loud.

In the morning, I did some yoga. Florence emerged two or three hours later and we walked to the shops for some food for breakfast. I felt that the conversation was a bit 'stilted', not a lot to say. Maybe I was outstaying my welcome but Florence, who is vegetarian, bought bacon for an English breakfast for me, and fruit for her, and some coffee too. I cooked my own and made a good job of both it and the coffee, fortunately. I didn't let the side down.

Florence had invited me for a walk, along with Sarah, but this was cancelled. Sarah wanted to talk privately. I felt slightly put down, not because of Florence but because of Sarah. I would have liked to see her.

Never mind – I could go home early.

When I left, I got several kisses on the cheek. This was significant. Last night Sarah, Florence and I had discussed the French manner of kissing on the cheek. Before she went to bed, I said to Florence that I would like to kiss her in an English way. She rejected that and said that kissing on the lips is for Russians and the English. For the French it has a deeper meaning. I'm not sure I understand – maybe one day.

So, kisses at leaving time were important to me. I got more than two! And I think they were more than 'polite goodbyes'. "See you soon," she said.

IF

If you would like me to love you
I will
If you cannot enter my life
I won't
If the time is yet to come
I will
'If' is not a question
'I will' is not an answer